CONCEPTUALIZING QUALITATIVE INQUIRY

Mindwork for Fieldwork in Education and the Social Sciences

Thomas H. Schram
University of New Hampshire

Merrill
Prentice Hall

Upper Saddle River, New Jersey
Columbus, Ohio

Vice President and Publisher: Jeffery W. Johnston
Executive Editor: Kevin M. Davis
Editorial Assistant: Autumn Crisp
Production Editor: Mary Harlan
Production Coordination: Lea Baranowski, Carlisle Publishers Services
Design Coordinator: Diane C. Lorenzo
Cover Design: Jason Moore
Cover Image: Corbis Stock Market
Text Design and Illustrations: Carlisle Publishers Services
Production Manager: Laura Messerly
Director of Marketing: Ann Castel Davis
Marketing Manager: Amy June
Marketing Coordinator: Tyra Cooper

This book was set in Garamond by Carlisle Communications, Ltd. It was printed and bound by R. R. Donnelley & Sons Company. The cover was printed by Phoenix Color Corp.

Pearson Education Ltd.
Pearson Education Australia Pty. Limited
Pearson Education Singapore Pte. Ltd.
Pearson Education North Asia Ltd.
Pearson Education Canada, Ltd.
Pearson Educación de Mexico, S.A. de C.V.
Pearson Education—Japan
Pearson Education Malaysia Pte. Ltd.
Pearson Education, *Upper Saddle River, New Jersey*

10 9 8 7 6 5 4 3 2 1
ISBN: 0-13-026336-2

For Cindy, Cody, and Jesse

PREFACE

Truth be known, the real work of qualitative research lies in mindwork, not fieldwork.

Harry F. Wolcott (2001, p. 96)

How to move yourself and your ideas through the process of conceptualizing and proposing a field-based qualitative study is the focus of this book. The text evolved, naturally and over time, from the questions and concerns of students trying to make sense of an experience that resists a neat and tidy definition. It has emerged, not as a source of clean or conclusive answers, but as a means to address practical questions and formulate your own judgments about how to proceed as a qualitative researcher.

QUESTIONING THROUGH COMPLEXITY

My approach in this text is to emphasize the conceptual underpinnings of field-based inquiry among social scientists and educational researchers, but to do so from the perspective of graduate students and others who are trying their hand at qualitative research for the first time. This approach bears some caution. Any attempt to deliver what a text like this promises risks reducing the complexity of thinking about, justifying, and engaging in field-based research to a series of how-to offerings. Some reduction is inevitable in the shift from lived experience to written text, but my aim is not to work *around* or *in spite of* complexity, but to *question through* the complexity that pursuit of the qualitative entails.

To this end, I have deliberately positioned the questions, frustrations, and anxieties of novice researchers in the foreground of the text. My goal is to catch real people at teachable moments, to focus on essential concepts and questions that reveal their significance in episodes that challenge the hows and whys of their efforts. Noticeably absent are the pristine and polished offerings of "old hands" whose exemplary monographs and journal articles—while something to aspire to—are often too far removed from the student more immediately concerned with how hunch begets problem begets question begets worthwhile study (or, for that matter, how to respond to all those professors who keep asking, "So, what's your theory?").

THE MATTER OF CONCEPTUALIZING

The matter of *conceptualizing,* to which the book's title refers, reflects a twofold emphasis. First, there is a procedural emphasis that regards conceptualizing as an essential prelude to the formulation of a workable and worthwhile field study. How do you transform hunches or personal concerns into something that can drive a purposeful inquiry? Correspondingly, how do you develop a mind-set that is conducive to good research? This emphasis underscores what Wolcott (1995) describes as the critical component for research, namely, "the ability to conceive, or to generate, the ideas that prompt and guide inquiry" (p. 178). This aspect of conceptualizing, the clarifying *mindwork*[1] that precedes and informs a research proposal and the start of fieldwork, is the primary emphasis throughout this text.

Second, there is conceptualizing in the sense of organizing one's thinking around selected orienting concepts. Examples include addressing the basic conceptual concerns of *focus* and *locus* as a means to clarify your research purposes (Chapter 2); drawing upon concepts of *authority, ownership, purposefulness,* and *credibility* to formulate an argument for your study (Chapter 4); or considering your approach to fieldwork through the lens of fundamental concepts such as *intent, involvement, familiarity,* and *role awareness* (Chapter 7). My aim is to use such concepts as a means to translate the multifaceted dialogue that is research into practical matters of application and choice about how to proceed as a researcher.

POSITIONING THE TEXT

Perspective, suggests anthropologist James Peacock (1986), is a matter of questioning both *how* one sees and how *one* sees. I have written this text from the perspective of one whose own introduction to qualitative inquiry reflected an acute awareness that what a researcher chooses to attend to, and how, is necessarily a trade-off in considering other matters of concern and ways of attending. This awareness is coupled with an understanding that qualitative research requires not only practical strategies for how to pursue an inquiry but also particular standards for what is worth knowing and how that knowledge is to be applied.

Together, these ideas direct attention to the premise that no single perspective encompasses the variety of viewpoints, practices, and traditions that are conveyed by the label *qualitative inquiry,* except at a general level. As I will address in Chapter 1, certain major themes and concepts recur in the understandings set forth by qualitatively oriented researchers, and these can helpfully (if not exhaustively) convey some of what it means to claim a qualitative stance.

Field-Oriented

As someone coming to qualitative research from the social sciences, I have, by training and inclination, a different perspective than those coming to qualitative research from, say, the arts and humanities. Fieldwork, in particular, would not necessarily be

---

[1] As far as I have been able to determine, use of the term *mindwork* in the context of qualitative research was coined, or at least popularized, by Harry Wolcott (1995), who stressed, "Fieldwork is a state of mind. And something you put your mind to. Whatever goes on in your mind as you prepare for it, engage in it, reflect back on it, and report from it, constitutes its essence" (p. 155). I have highlighted the term for this text to emphasize the importance of your mental set as you anticipate and prepare for fieldwork.

a defining characteristic of inquiry for those approaching research from an aesthetic or philosophical perspective. This book focuses on the significant proportion of qualitative pathways within the social sciences that are field-oriented and that involve actual interactions with people and experiences in natural settings.

Depth over Breadth

In providing illustrations for the conceptual core of the text, I have purposefully emphasized depth over breadth. My decision to attend to certain research perspectives and traditions but not others boils down to the priority I place on conceptual clarity rather than methodological comprehensiveness. My aim in Chapters 3 and 6, for example, is not to account for a range of approaches but to clarify how particular approaches predispose you to see things in particular ways and position you to achieve certain aims. Coming to terms with how this positioning might play out in one or two instances provides a basis, or at least a point of comparison, for understanding how it might play out in others.

In complementary fashion I draw upon specific questions and examples from students with whom I have worked, as well as a few from my own research. The primary experiential thread that serves to connect Chapters 2 through 9 is represented by Patrice, a student whose initial foray into qualitative research reflects the types of steps and stumbles encountered by newcomers to the field. Her preliminary drafts, thoughtful insights, and honest appraisal of her evolving inquiry provide a cumulative and in-depth means to explore the process of conceptualizing a study.

My own graduate-level courses in qualitative design, ethnography, field methods, and the like are based in education, but over the past 12 years or so have included students from sociology, anthropology, family studies, nursing, social work, natural resources, and more. Most of the examples in the text are drawn from the experiences of students engaged in research in education, the social sciences, and the delivery of social services, but the ideas addressed are not limited to the needs of students, scholars, and practitioners in these fields.

Voice

The issue of voice is pivotal in qualitative inquiry in that it expresses one's stance relative to the distance and the relationship between researcher and researched, and between author and reader. I write throughout the book in a voice and tone reflective of the directness and candor that I seek to foster in discussions with my students and advisees. I directly engage you, the reader, much as you would hear me talking with students about their research while seated around a table in a seminar room, in my office, or in the local coffee shop. Conceptualizing an inquiry, like fieldwork itself, is a human endeavor in which personal contact and straight talk can carry you further along than academic posturing and heaped jargon. You cannot, of course, discuss qualitative inquiry without encountering some pretty heady notions, and there are many in the chapters that follow. It is my intent to bring you to a practical understanding of these notions by revealing how they pertain to people who have faced the types of questions and difficulties you likely face as a newcomer to the field.

ORGANIZATION OF THE CHAPTERS

The chapters that follow are organized in ways that reflect my dual commitment to convey the iterative and interconnected nature of conceptualizing and designing a qualitative study and to consider particular aspects of that process in depth. I do not treat in detail either the deeper historical or theoretical underpinnings of qualitative inquiry or the actual carrying out of a fieldwork project after the proposal stage. Rather, this text complements existing overviews of research foundations and methods by looking specifically at practical issues involved in conceiving and connecting the ideas that prompt and guide a qualitative study.

I use as my point of entry a broad brushstroke characterization of qualitative inquiry as a complex and contested work in progress. Chapter 1 sorts through competing assumptions and recurring themes in qualitative inquiry, ultimately building a case for the distinctive contributions that enable researchers to claim they are proceeding from a qualitative stance.

The chapters in Part One, Positioning Yourself for Inquiry, narrow the scope of discussion and direct attention to discrete aspects of conceptualizing and generating a study. Chapter 2 works through the initial complexity of positioning yourself relative to a researchable problem and clarifying your intent in doing so. Chapter 3 poses both guidelines and challenges tied to the construction of your intellectual orientation and moral stance as a researcher. Chapter 4 addresses the fundamental assumption of coherence that underlies all your efforts, and discusses how you might make a case for how and why your ideas matter relative to the work and ideas of others. Moving your inquiry toward a point of clear definition in the form of a research question is the focus of Chapter 5. Chapter 6, the concluding chapter in Part One, presents strategies for determining when and how it matters to distinguish your approach as a particular type of field-based research.

The chapters in Part Two focus on the need to anticipate aspects of your inquiry in action. Chapter 7 presents a number of strategic considerations that address whether you are *in* place and in the *right* place to pursue field-based inquiry. Chapter 8 prepares you to respond to the practical and ethical issues involved in establishing the integrity and ultimate trustworthiness of your study.

The multiple dimensions of conceptualizing a study find expression in specific parts of a research proposal, the actual document that you construct to communicate and justify to a particular audience how you have conceptualized your inquiry (Maxwell, 1996). Chapter 9 highlights how you might draw upon elements of your conceptualizing work to inform and shape a written proposal for your study.

ACKNOWLEDGMENTS

My acknowledgments begin where this book began, with my students in EDUC 904, Qualitative Inquiry in Education, along with the masters and doctoral students I have advised in the course of their research. Special thanks to Patrice Hallock, who shares the details of her experiences with the highs and lows of research in the pages of this book. Patrice also provided thoughtful and thorough feedback on various manuscript drafts. For their contributions in various ways to the content and format of this book I also wish to thank Timothy Gutmann, Gretchen Hanser, Antonio Henley, Deborah Jameson, Cari Moorhead, Julie Newman, Carina Self, Althea Sheaff, Carolyn Shepard, Betsey Stebbins, and Rosemary Zurawel.

I would like to thank the reviewers of this manuscript, who invested valuable time and generated thoughtful critique during the development of this book. These reviewers include James H. Banning, Colorado State University; Donald Blumenfeld-Jones, Arizona State University; David Flinders, Indiana University; Peter A. Hessling, North Carolina State University; Barbara Kawulich, Georgia State University and Mercer University; Joseph Maxwell, George Mason University; Maria Piantanida, University of Pittsburgh; Marcia L. Rosal, Florida State University; and Michelle D. Young, University of Missouri. Coming to terms with qualitative inquiry is an inherently argumentative and incomplete process, and I am grateful to these individuals for their insightful and balanced perspectives. The responsibility for any misperceptions or shortcomings in the text is entirely my own.

I would also like to acknowledge the wonderful staff at Merrill/Prentice Hall who ushered the book along with grace, skill, and professionalism. In particular, I wish to thank Kevin Davis, Executive Editor, for believing in my ideas and in my writing; Autumn Crisp, Editorial Assistant, for her enthusiastic support and attention to detail; Lea Baranowski, Project Editor at Carlisle Publishers Services, for her remarkable communication skills and organizational savvy; and Karen Bankston, copy editor, for affirming my voice while honing my presentation.

I was originally drawn into this project through the encouragement and collaborative energy of my good friend and colleague, Geoff Mills (Southern Oregon University). He has remained a steady source of advice and feedback throughout the development of this book, and I am deeply indebted to him. I would also like to thank my friend and mentor, Harry Wolcott, for his editorial assistance and detailed comments on an earlier draft of the manuscript.

Finally, for their help in countless ways, including generous portions of patience and good humor, I thank my sons, Cody and Jesse. For keeping all of us focused on what's important and for her enduring love and support, I thank, foremost and always, my wife, Cindy.

Tom Schram

Brief Contents

CONTENTS

CHAPTER 1

CLAIMING THE QUALITATIVE IN YOUR INQUIRY

> Where is my point of entry into qualitative inquiry? What underlies the claim that I might be proceeding as a qualitative researcher? What sort of mind-set contributes to my ability to proceed from a qualitative stance? What do qualitative researchers have in common? How do features of qualitative inquiry inform the way I might conceptualize a study?

FINDING A POINT OF ENTRY

As eager as I am to engage you in thinking about how to proceed with a qualitative inquiry, I must begin with a note of caution. "Claiming the qualitative" is not an advisable starting point for your efforts as a researcher, suggesting as it does that your decision about *how* to proceed is prerequisite to decisions about *why, where, around what concerns,* and *from what perspective* you are proceeding. As a point of entry for this book, however, it serves a number of useful aims.

In starting with a broad view of qualitative inquiry, I hope to establish a means for you to place the parts that follow in context. My implicit aim, reflective of a qualitative bent, is to invite consideration of how parts and whole interact in a way that presents the process of conceptualizing an inquiry as more, rather than less, complex. The chapters in Part One will get you working from the ground up soon enough, directing your attention to discrete aspects of generating a study. For now, let the broad brush strokes of this chapter serve as a reminder that you can never really attend to any one aspect of the inquiry process in isolation from the others and without an appreciation of the big picture.

The view of qualitative inquiry presented in this first chapter highlights these key points:

- Qualitative inquiry is a work in progress.
- There is no one best way to be a qualitative researcher.
- We cannot usefully discuss how to do qualitative research without attending to competing assumptions about how qualitative research can and should be done.
- Recurring themes in qualitative inquiry enable us to speak of its distinctive contributions.
- These distinctive contributions can inform the way we conceptualize and generate a study.

ENGAGING IN QUALITATIVE CONVERSATIONS

> We find neither definite nor conclusive answers to the question of what makes a qualitative study qualitative. Like a friend's face in a crowd, we recognize a qualitative study when we see one; its features seem unmistakable, but few of us can explain why. That familiar face, the melody of a song, or the aroma of food are among the many aspects of everyday life that we learn to recognize from repeated, firsthand experience. Our knowledge is largely tacit, and so, it would seem, is our knowledge of qualitative research. (Flinders & Mills, 1993, p. xi)

One point on which most researchers would agree is that qualitative inquiry is much more difficult to define than it is simply to identify. The myriad forms of qualitative research—each with its own perspective, conventions, disciplinary alliances, and internal divisions—leave many of those who seek a common defining thread in a state of despair. The task is akin to entering a crowded room and trying to listen in on a number of ongoing conversations. How do you decide where you should focus your attention? What are the consequences of listening in on just one conversation to the exclusion of others? What if one circle of talk sets you up to be at odds with the one right next to it? What conversations are you likely to encounter, and what can you learn from them?

The labeling conversation.   As you edge toward this conversation, it appears a comfortable enough place to start. It is relatively straightforward, you reason, to draw distinctions among various types of qualitative research—certainly more so than to define qualitative inquiry as any sort of coherent whole. Then you get your first earful and realize that this conversation is not unlike opening Pandora's box. Some of the terms being tossed around appear to be synonymous or to overlap with others; other terms that are used in tandem are not on the same conceptual level. Still others that you had assumed to be popular fail to meet criteria as an actual qualitative "type" according to one viewpoint or another.

You step back and consider the possibilities. A qualitative research designation may refer to a perspective ("interpretive," "naturalistic"), a disciplinary tradition ("ethnography," "phenomenology"), an epistemological stance ("feminist," "hermeneutic"), a type of strategy ("participant observation," "focus group"), or even a location ("field study"). Given such a range of possibilities, at what conceptual level do you compare, for example, a feminist study and a grounded theory study? For that matter, how should you regard a designation like *grounded theory,* which can be considered both a set of assumptions about the production of knowledge and a set of guidelines for data collection and analysis? And what about the eclectic *case study*—is it better regarded as a strategy for conducting research (Merriam, 1998; Stake, 1995; Yin, 1994) or simply as a form of reporting (Wolcott, 1992, 2001)?

Adding to this complexity is the common practice among researchers of combining perspectives. For example, you could do a critical ethnography, combining elements of ethnography and critical theory. Or you could apply a postmodern feminist lens to a grounded theory study, as one of my students did, designating the components of her approach as methodological (grounded theory) and philosophical (postmodern feminist).

In short, more is at stake in this part of the crowded room than simply the sorting and labeling of methods and strategies. What you can draw from this qualitative conversation is an awareness of the choices that surround you and an appreciation of how these choices express oppositions as well as agreements.[1]

The disciplinary conversation.   You wander over to this conversation as you hear the familiar names of well-established disciplines. Sociology, anthropology, psychology, history, socio-linguistics, and so on all promote their own traditions of qualitative inquiry, often with identifiable favorites to which researchers are drawn. But disciplinary border work starts to complicate matters of definition and distinction. Ethnography, for example, although grounded in anthropology, has held sway in educational circles for years. It continues to do so, retaining many of its distinctive anthropological features, but is now making room for narrative inquiry, to which at least five disciplines lay claim (Clandinin & Connelly, 2000; Cortazzi, 1993).

At another level of disciplinary border work, you may encounter an exchange in which the terms *interpretivist, constructivist, phenomenological,* and *naturalistic* are bantered about in synonymous fashion, reflecting one or another's grounding in sociology, philosophy, or anthropology. Such examples of overlap and similarity abound across disciplinary lines. The good news is that this qualitative conversation is typically characterized less by discord than by polite (but perhaps still pointed) acknowledgment of differences.

The postmodern conversation.   Intriguing claims of advocacy and self-appraisal draw your attention here, as well as the critical questioning of terms used to describe what researchers are actually up to in their work. Qualitative researchers of all types have responded in various ways (including feeling lost, as you might at first) to ethical and representational challenges posed by the *postmodern* context. This tends to be a lively interdisciplinary conversation, reflecting wide disagreement as to what exactly the term *postmodern* means, except perhaps that it represents a reaction to, critique of, or departure from conventional styles of academic discourse rooted in so-called "modernism" (Schwandt, 1997).

Your easiest point of entry for this conversation might be in assessing postmodernism's impact rather than ascertaining its precise meaning. For example, postmodern influences have directed more explicit attention to how local and global concerns are linked together as well as how individuals can be linked morally and

---

[1] Some qualitative scholars, notably Tesch (1990) and Patton (2002), have generated detailed explanations of qualitative research types. Tesch's typology groups the various types of qualitative research within four areas of research interest: characteristics of language, discovery of regularities, discerning meaning, and reflection. Patton, in contrast, summarizes 16 common theoretical and philosophical perspectives that can inform qualitative inquiry. An especially helpful aspect of Patton's work is the identification of central questions that provide the focus of inquiry for each of the perspectives.

practically in the collaborative construction of a research agenda and product. The postmodern attitude has also prompted researchers to debate the basis for the authority of qualitative research claims, including how and to what end researchers can represent others in their studies. Researchers are now challenged to communicate how their perspectives and actions, and those of study participants, express social, political, and moral values (Schwandt, 2000).

Fundamentally, the postmodern conversation is about the positioning of inquiry and the inquirer amidst contradictory and complicated issues of power, ownership of knowledge, and political and economic contexts. To whatever degree you become actively engaged in this conversation, it is a good idea to keep an ear attuned to it as a way to position your own inquiry within the broader qualitative dialogue. (For insightful discussions of qualitative inquiry in the postmodern era, see Denzin, 1997; Dickens & Fontana, 1994; and Esteva & Prakash, 1998.)

The moral conversation.   Either branching out from the postmodern conversation or emerging on its own as one of the focal points for discussion among qualitative researchers today is the question of what ethics in research is all about (de Laine, 2000; Lincoln, 1995). Everyone in the room finds reason to contribute to this exchange of ideas at some point. The trend in contemporary fieldwork toward more participation and less observation is making it an especially problematic but necessary conversation in which to be engaged.

As you enter this circle of talk, be prepared to confront dilemmas, not simply about the consequences of looking at study participants but also the responsibilities tied to being with and even for them (Denzin, 1997). This prospect can be particularly intimidating to the newcomer, reflecting as it does a broadening of the ethical conversation from traditional, easily codified concerns about what researchers might *do* to study participants (raising issues of informed consent and confidentiality, for example) to the moral implications of simply being a researcher (Kellehear, 1993). Chapters 3 and 8 will revisit some of the implications of this conversation for your work in establishing both an intellectual identity and moral presence as a researcher.

The dichotomizing conversation.   In a recent commentary on the tendency of many researchers to establish either/or positions, Watkins (2001) draws upon this instructive paradox: "Actually, there *are* two kinds of people in this world: those who believe there are two kinds of people in this world and those who are smart enough to know better" (quoting from Robbins, 1980, p. 82). In highlighting our very human inclination to make everything dichotomous, this paradox directs attention to what is arguably the least productive type of conversation in our crowded qualitative room. It is so frustrating because it is often not a conversation at all, but rather, to use Watkin's terms, a "talking past each other."

I confront this issue most every day. When students and colleagues describe me as "you know, a qualitative type," I am left to wonder how accurately those prefacing words "*you* know" reflect agreement that we *all* know what we are talking about. Employing the designation "qualitative type" to mean simply that one is not a quantitative type usually leaves those in the qualitative camp to be defined by what they're not or defensive about what others say they should be.

You have to decide how useful this type of talk is for defining what you are up to as a researcher. For example, does the characteristically qualitative engagement with notions of subjectivity obligate you to discount objectivity at any level, or are there ways to consider how both notions inform your thinking? What are you willing to claim about distinctions between *understanding* and *action* as aims of inquiry? What about distinctions between researcher and researched? The lesson from this conversation is to regard either/or pronouncements with a discerning eye. In each instance where a dichotomy might be constructed, keep in mind the potential offered by defining your place outside as well as inside its lines of definition.

Cautions and Questions from Qualitative Conversations

My advice to students and novice researchers, mirroring that offered by Wolcott (1995), is to be "informed as to the substance of these debates rather than to be drawn prematurely into them" (p. 159). Do not feel pressed to come up with "the answer," if there is such a thing regarding these matters. *Do* prepare yourself sufficiently to convey a "thoughtful position" (Wolcott, 1995), at least with respect to how the issue at hand might pertain to your particular inquiry.

When you engage in any or all of the preceding qualitative conversations in the course of reading, class discussion, and your own preliminary steps toward field-work, you will naturally come to view a particular approach as a preferred way of conducting research. Such choice amidst variety is the spice of the qualitative life, but it also precludes a generic vision that could be labeled as *the* qualitative approach. So what *do* qualitative researchers have in common? And what might underlie the claim that your approach to inquiry is qualitative?

CHOOSING TO THINK QUALITATIVELY

Your eventual choice of a preferred way of conducting inquiry will reveal in some measure the professional socialization you have undergone in your graduate studies—that is, the ideas, perspectives, and people to whom you are exposed. It will also reflect a case-by-case determination of what is an appropriate approach (a "good fit") for the research questions you are pursuing (see Chapters 5 and 6). At a more implicit level, the way you choose to proceed as a researcher will reflect your natural and acquired predispositions, the mind-set you bring to the task of inquiry.

Start now to identify and acknowledge the fundamental inclinations that inform your decisions about inquiry. Ask yourself: Am I predisposed as a researcher toward achieving some sort of closure, toward seeking knowledge that can be replicated and reconfirmed and therefore held with considerable certainty? Is it important that my data enable me to explain, predict, or even control the outcomes of similar future events? Am I uncomfortable with uncertainty?

Alternatively, while acknowledging the need for some level of assurance, ask yourself: Am I more inclined toward uncovering multiple (sometimes even conflicting) interpretations of the phenomenon or experience that I am investigating? Am I comfortable with the prospect of furnishing more than a single meaning to features of an experience? Am I predisposed toward the generation of questions that invite rather than reduce complexity? Am I comfortable with uncertainty?

The first grouping of questions reflects the degree to which qualitative inquiry is still responding to the "science" in the social sciences (Page, 2000). "Yes" responses to those first several questions suggest that you might yet be uncomfortable challenging some of the positivist tendencies of that science. Affirmative responses to the second grouping of questions reflect, in rather broad terms, a predisposition to think in qualitative terms. Do not worry; this is not a test of your viability as a qualitative researcher. Think of it more as an initial positioning of yourself along a continuum that encompasses the varying tendencies and emphases that each of us brings to the process of inquiry.

A Qualitative Predisposition

As a qualitative researcher your position on the continuum will indicate a predisposition toward working *with* and *through* complexity rather than *around* or *in spite of* it. You will embrace the challenge of turning familiar facts and understandings into puzzles. You will see value in seeking out your subjectivity as a means to explore how your assumptions and personal biography may be shaping your inquiry and its outcomes. From an enlarged awareness of how your own assumptions may be informing or affecting your understanding will emerge a still greater appreciation of complexity.

You will undertake inquiry not so much to achieve closure in the form of definitive answers to problems but rather to generate questions that raise fresh, often critical awareness and understanding of problems. Your distinctive contribution will lie in raising questions about ideas otherwise taken for granted or left unasked (Barone, 2001; Page, 2000).

In this way you might begin to identify yourself as a qualitative researcher: embracing complexity, uncovering and challenging taken-for-granted assumptions, feeling comfortable knowing your direction but not necessarily your destination. If we view the nature of qualitative inquiry in these terms, it becomes even more apparent that, while there are numerous ways to construct qualitative understanding, there is no one way to be a qualitative researcher. What, then, can we add that allows us to group a range of approaches and methodologies under the rubric *qualitative*?

PROCEEDING FROM A QUALITATIVE STANCE

To speak of qualitative inquiry as being coherent, as most of us instinctively do, is not to claim that its practitioners are the same, know the same things, use the same methods, or ask the same types of questions. Instead, the coherence of qualitative inquiry finds form in the suggestion that those who are committed to it share an understanding that certain issues are pivotal in the conduct of their research. The dialogue around these concerns has been a defining one in that it has cultivated an awareness of key features and assumptions that distinguish what it means to proceed from a qualitative stance.

In a commentary on the evolution of qualitative inquiry across disciplines, Page (2000) notes distinctive features of qualitative methodology that appear to have been retained over the years:

> . . . chiefly a research focus on "one human being trying to figure out what some others are up to" (Agar, 1996, p. 2), the ancient and seemingly ordinary method of fieldwork, and a research logic that is both empirical *and* imaginative as it works to portray how people are simultaneously unique and connected, often in ways they only partially comprehend. (p. 28)

Building upon these basic notions, we can portray the perspective of qualitative inquiry writ large as grounded in assumptions about the social world, and implications of those assumptions for field-based research, that include the following.

Guiding Assumptions of Qualitative Inquiry

- **We gain understanding of the social world through direct personal experiences in real-world settings.**

What this means for you as a qualitative researcher:
    Qualitative inquiry finds its strength in the opportunities made possible by being there and getting close to people and circumstances, either through physical proximity and participation over time or in the social sense of shared experience, empathy, and confidentiality (Patton, 2002). The focus of a qualitative study unfolds naturally in that it has no predetermined course established or manipulated by the researcher such as would occur in a laboratory or other controlled setting. Researchers get personally engaged where the action is and in a way that draws upon all their senses, including, as Patton (2002, p. 49) emphasizes, "the capacity to experience affect no less than cognition."
    To immerse yourself in naturally occurring complexity calls for your ability to let go of control of possible confounding variables (for example, who in the setting is willing to talk to you about particular issues) and to expect and be prepared to go with the flow of changing circumstances. In keeping with an approach that at various times has been described as naturalistic or discovery-oriented, you engage study participants as much as possible in places and under conditions that are comfortable for and familiar to them (Patton, 2002). Correspondingly, and in contrast to a laboratory setting, it is more often the study participants rather than the researcher who dictate the timing and tone of interactions. Being open and pragmatic to this degree requires that you possess a high comfort level with ambiguity and uncertainty as well as trust in the ultimate value of what an emergent and largely inductive analytical process will provide (see "Working Inductively . . . or Not" in Chapter 2).

- **In pursuing inquiry into the social world we need to acknowledge the quintessentially interactive and intersubjective nature of constructing knowledge.**

What this means for you as a qualitative researcher:

Developing qualitative understanding through field-based research means that you engage in personal encounters and exchanges with self and others. Simply stated, qualitative methods work through you. Your presence, manifested through talking, listening, looking, reading, and reflecting in greater or lesser degrees of engagement with study participants, filters and affects what counts as meaningful knowledge for your inquiry.[2] Several essential aspects of qualitative fieldwork frame these considerations (Glesne, 1999; Patton, 2002; Rossman & Rallis, 1998):

- The perspectives and subjective lenses that the researcher and research participants bring to a qualitative study are part of the context for the findings.
- The negotiation of research relationships is ongoing, with the potential for the perspectives and understandings of both researcher and participants to be changed in the course of the inquiry. Part of your responsibility is to monitor and account for how these changes influence your fieldwork and interpretation of events.
- Developing self-awareness—that is, examining *what I know* and *how I know it*—is essential to determining the influence of research relationships on your inquiry and to constructing an authentic understanding of what's going on.

Together, these considerations point toward an acquired sensitivity, a simultaneous awareness of self and other and of the interplay between the two, that has become a defining feature of qualitative inquiry. Typically conveyed by the term *reflexivity,* this self-questioning reminds the qualitative inquirer that making perspectives and assumptions explicit serves to inform, not undermine, a study's credibility. How do I know what I know? How do study participants know what they know? How do I perceive them? How do they perceive me, and how might they respond to my interpretations? How and why is that important? These types of questions define part of the work of qualitative inquiry and affirm the centrality of real, live, individual human beings in that work.

Chapter 7's consideration of involvement and Chapter 8's discussion of presence, selectivity, and subjectivity provide an opportunity to revisit these issues in the context of decisions you will face as you prepare for fieldwork.

- **Inquiry into the social world calls for sensitivity to context.**

What this means for you as a qualitative researcher:

Qualitative inquirers seek to make phenomena more complex, not simpler. For this reason, qualitative research is context sensitive or context specific—that is, it proceeds from the assumption that ideas, people, and events cannot be fully understood if isolated from the circumstances in which and through which they naturally occur.

---

[2] I deliberately avoid describing this in terms of the *self as research instrument,* the phrase of choice among researchers for many years now. Self as instrument tends to convey making use of the self simply as a means to an end, particularly in the sense of imposing oneself on or applying oneself to a situation.

As Patton (2002) instructively reminds us, "taking something out of context" is to distort it, to change its meaning by omitting consideration of how a gesture, a conversation, or even a word occurs in a context that locates it in time, space, and circumstance. The scientific or quantitative ideal of generalizing across time and space places a premium on identifying qualities or "truths" that do not depend on context. Qualitative inquiry, in contrast, preserves natural context. This means that, as qualitative researchers, we are not in the business of separating out variables or taking things apart to see how they work. Rather, we are in the business of embedding, of putting things in relation to the larger set of circumstances of which they are a part.

- **Inquiry into the social world calls for attentiveness to particulars.**

What this means for you as a qualitative researcher:

At first glance, attentiveness to particulars might seem an odd conceptual companion to qualitative inquiry's emphasis on context, but a second look reveals their complementary positions as two sides of the same coin. Anthropologist Clifford Geertz (1973) coined the wonderful term *complex specificness* to convey the understanding that a researcher's findings can be both specific and circumstantial. In this light, the complexity we seek to uncover as qualitative inquirers is understood by attending to the particular (and unpredictable) nature of events or cases, rather than to their general character and overall distribution. Depth, richness, and detail provide the basis for a qualitative account's claim to relevance in some broader context.

For several years in the early 1990s I undertook a study of Laotian refugee students in a rural high school that accounted for the experiences and perspectives of scores of disparate family, school, community, and public agency members within the portrayal of a single case. In confronting the "complex specificness" of a particular teacher's experience with a particular group of students, I presented a means to think realistically and concretely *about* broader problems of cross-cultural adjustment, home-school relationships, and the like. This is not a claim to see the world in a grain of sand, but a characteristically qualitative acknowledgment that small aspects of experience, conveyed in depth and detail, can speak to large issues.

- **Qualitative inquiry is fundamentally interpretive.**

What this means for you as a qualitative researcher:

Experiences do not speak for themselves; nor do features within a research setting directly or spontaneously announce themselves as worthy of your attention. As a qualitative fieldworker, you cannot view your task simply as a matter of gathering or generating "facts" about "what happened." Rather, you engage in an active process of *interpretation:* noting some things as significant, noting but ignoring others as not significant, and missing other potentially significant things altogether (see Chapter 8's discussion of presence, interpretive necessity, and selectivity).

Consider the deceptively straightforward task of transcribing a taped interview. Given the common lack of clear-cut endings in ordinary speech, how do you determine when and how to punctuate to indicate a completed phrase or sentence? Is it a function of *how* the interviewee said what she said? How do you determine *how* something was said? How does your decision affect the intent or meaning of what was actually spoken? And ultimately, how do you determine the degree of trust you should attach to what was said? In other words, even a transcript is the product of ongoing interpretive (and ethical) decisions about the significance that you give to what other people convey as meaningful.

Interpretation, following Peshkin (2000), means building upon assumptions of fact (what you and others perceive and select as important and meaningful in what you are learning) and incorporating them into a line of reasoning (interconnecting what you are learning with other actions or circumstances). The credibility of your interpretation, Peshkin suggests, rests on others seeing and accepting the relationship between your facts and your reasoning—a matter of persuasion, not proof. And because you conduct your research from some point of view, other interpretations and understandings are possible and may compete with your own.

These considerations point to the fundamental assumption that qualitative inquiry is not a search for knowledge for knowledge's sake (or for knowledge that is simply "out there"), but a search for the *significance* of knowledge (Edson, 1988). In this sense, interpretation really has nothing to do with proving things right or wrong, predicting, or controlling. Interpretation demonstrates its worth through its explanatory power and its capacity to impact or inspire the practice of others (Peshkin, 2000; Wolcott, 1994).

Keeping Matters in Perspective

I caution you to keep these general assumptions and qualities in perspective. On the one hand, they are not absolutely definitive in the sense that they say all there is to say about a qualitative stance. On the other hand, all that they say does not account for the fact that when people use the designation *qualitative inquiry,* they can mean very different things depending on the qualitative conversations to which they are most attuned. With this mind-set we start to come to terms with how we define ourselves as qualitative researchers: walking together on separate, sometimes overlapping paths, recognizing that we address concerns differently but appreciating the fact that we have common concerns to address.

USING QUALITIES TO INFORM CONCEPTUALIZATION

Immersing yourself in naturally occurring complexity. Acknowledging the interactive and intersubjective nature of your sense making. Proceeding with sensitivity to context. Attending to particulars. Employing an interpretive frame of reference. All of these qualities and considerations find expression through the process of conceptualizing and generating a qualitative study (as well as in the subsequent conduct and presentation of the research). As we proceed through the chapters of this book, we will see how each quality finds particular definition and significance within discrete aspects of the conceptualization process.

Table 1.1 provides a way to view how the qualities described in the previous section find emphasis in the particular tasks and processes described in Chapters 2

Table 1.1

Qualitative Features Informing Conceptualization

Qualitative Feature	Finds Particular Emphasis in. . .
Direct personal experience in real-world settings	Problem finding and entry-level theorizing *(Chapter 2)* Clarifying your practical purposes *(Chapter 2)*
Interactive and intersubjective nature	Considering ways of being a researcher *(Chapter 3)* Anticipating fieldwork strategies *(Chapter 7)* Establishing practical and ethical integrity *(Chapter 8)*
Sensitivity to context	Situating the problem *(Chapter 2)* Constructing a conceptual context *(Chapter 4)*
Attentiveness to particulars	Distinguishing focus and locus *(Chapter 2)* Clarifying your research purposes *(Chapter 2)* Forming research questions *(Chapter 5)*
Interpretive nature	Making decisions about methodological distinctions *(Chapter 6)* Anticipating fieldwork strategies *(Chapter 7)* Establishing practical and ethical integrity *(Chapter 8)*

through 8. I realize that using a table to display how qualities are expressed within particular processes may oversimplify matters, particularly in terms of suggesting clearly defined one-to-one relationships. Keep in mind that this table is not a representation of absolute or exclusive linkages, but a way to introduce the relative emphasis of qualities within and across features of conceptualization.

Consider, for illustration, the first feature displayed, that of direct personal experience in real-world settings. Although by no means limited to the concerns described in Chapter 2, the interplay and input of direct experience and personal concerns are especially significant in how you engage and shape a sense of problem and purpose for your inquiry. It is at this preliminary phase of problem finding and initial theorizing that firsthand knowledge and experience play a major role in your determination that "we have a problem" or "something is missing in my understanding of this situation."

In the subsequent delineation of the various aims of your inquiry, your direct personal experience likewise feeds substantially into the practical purposes of your research. These purposes, distinct from your researchable aims (see Chapter 2), pertain to real-life applications directed at change, improvement, or advocacy that your research will inform.

Again, keep in mind that all such considerations are matters of emphasis. Direct personal experience plays into nearly every facet of conceptualizing a qualitative study, as do the other features introduced in this chapter and portrayed in Table 1.1. For now I am merely drawing attention to topics upon which these features have an especially significant or defining influence. Taken together, the features and topics portrayed in Table 1.1 can provide points of reference to mark your progress through the chapters of this book.

SUMMARY

This chapter introduced qualitative inquiry as a complex and contested work in progress, an approach to research that is much more difficult to define than it is simply to identify. Its coherence rests upon persuasive principles and guiding assumptions rather than absolute rules and clear-cut distinctions. Accordingly, there is no single, agreed-upon way to "be" a qualitative researcher.

The decision to proceed from a qualitative stance reflects a predisposition toward working with and toward complexity, rather than seeking knowledge that can be replicated and reconfirmed. Qualitative researchers are careful about, even dubious of, the possibility or meaningfulness of generalization across time and circumstances. They see value in seeking out their subjectivity and exploring how their assumptions may be shaping their inquiry and its outcomes.

Although competing claims about how qualitative research can and should be done preclude a generic vision that could be labeled as *the* qualitative approach, several recurring themes enable us to speak of qualitative inquiry's distinctive features. These guiding themes or assumptions include a commitment to direct experiences with people, situations, and ideas as they naturally occur; an acknowledgment of the interactive and intersubjective nature of constructing knowledge; the need to be sensitive to context as a means to understand the complexity of phenomena; the value of attending to the particular, unpredictable, and complex nature of specific cases; and the logic and necessity of an interpretive frame of reference. As revealed in the chapters that follow, these assumptions find expression within and across the various dimensions of conceptualizing and generating a qualitative study.

PART ONE

POSITIONING YOURSELF FOR INQUIRY

A STRATEGY TO HOLD IT ALL TOGETHER

During the period of her graduate work in education Patrice directed an infant and toddler program that provided early intervention services to families in the state. Drawing upon her professional ties with Early Head Start programs throughout rural northern New England, she hoped to conduct a study of infant well-being from the perspectives of families impacted by poverty. Her preliminary research aims reflected a twofold emphasis, addressing both the concept of infant mental health and the experience of participation in a program that provided services for families with infants. Her following reflection describes the mix of, in her words, "giddy excitement" and "painful cognitive dissonance" that characterized the search for ways to conceptualize a research design.

> I began the semester seeking a way of conceptualizing my proposed study that was "solid," much like a scaffold or blueprint to a house. From the start, however, I was cautioned that I needed to take into account my changing understanding of concepts and that, if I visualized my framework for inquiry as a scaffold or similar image, it would likely be too rigid. "It's a dynamic process, not a static blueprint," I was reminded by my advisor. My discomfort around such a notion of research design rose rapidly—how could I hold on to something that was fluid?
>
> I looked to the literature on research design. My reading led me to identify sources for the "modules" of a theoretical framework: experiential knowledge, existing theory and research, pilot and exploratory research, and thought experiments (Maxwell, 1996). I revisited an exercise I completed for an earlier seminar that tracked the origins and evolution of my research perspective through the succession of proposed titles for my study (Peshkin, 1985). I systematically unpacked the "subjective I's" that were contributing to the shape and direction of my research ideas (Glesne & Peshkin, 1992; Peshkin, 1988). I completed a writing exercise in which I identified my biases, made explicit my identity and experience, and wrote an "experience memo" (Maxwell, 1996). I identified existing theory I was likely to draw on for my research, and I thought about how

I might use my ideological stance as part of a framework for my inquiry (Creswell, 1998). The pieces, as discrete entities, were beginning to make some sense, but my biggest challenge remained: How could I maintain the coherence of all of these elements in a way that allowed for the dynamic, changing process inherent in qualitative inquiry?

This was the point at which I realized I had been confusing my desire for a solid framework with a need for a strategy to hold it all together—a way to maintain coherence while allowing for fluidity. If I could come up with a way to visualize my research design, I would have a way spatially to organize myself. I needed a way to hold on to and organize the inquiry process so that I could pay attention to bits of it at a time and not lose sight of it as a whole. I likened my experience at this point to visiting an unfamiliar city, an adventure that I could enjoy as long as I knew where I was on the map. I needed a way to spatially represent the pieces of my research design, see where I was in relation to them, and find my way around the landscape of my inquiry.

THE DYNAMIC WITHIN THE DESIGN

Patrice's reflection provides a useful starting point for considering what is conveyed by the notion of *research design*. Her expressed need for a sense of coherence amid fluidity suggests a dynamic within the design process that is often glossed over by those seeking a straightforward and structured pattern for framing their inquiry.

Marshall and Rossman (1999) suggest the term *cycle of inquiry* to conceptualize one's design. They emphasize that researchers may begin—grab a hold of—the process by considering any of the personal, professional, and political influences that are motivating their inquiry. Patrice, for example, was driven by a deep emotional commitment to infants and an intrigue with her professional relationship as a middle class service provider working with families impacted by poverty—an interest she could trace back to particular memories of material differences among classmates during her primary school years.

In similar fashion, Maxwell (1996) emphasizes that research design does not begin from a fixed starting point or proceed through a predetermined sequence of steps. He describes an iterative and interactive process that is "compatible with the definition of design as the arrangement of elements governing the functioning of a study" (p. 4) and "in which each component of the design may need to be reconsidered or modified in response to . . . changes in some other component" (p. 2). One's research question, traditionally viewed as the necessary starting point for a design (Janesick, 1994; LeCompte & Schensul, 1999), is in this interactional way of thinking generally the *result* of a design process (Marshall & Rossman, 1999; Maxwell, 1996).

The basic premise underlying the five chapters in Part One plays off these notions and reflects what sociologist Howard Becker describes as a distinguishing feature of qualitative research, namely, that it is designed "in the making" (quoted in Wolcott, 1995, p.177). This notion suggests that qualitative researchers do not frame and follow a research design as much as they *orchestrate and clarify connections* among the various raw materials and thought-about perspectives that feed into their developing inquiry. Their task, in other words, is precisely the challenge identified by Patrice: to develop strategies for holding on to, making sense of, and forging links among the ideas that are prompting and guiding their inquiry.

In practice, giving shape and substance to a process that is designed "in the making" means that you are never really attending to any one aspect of that process in isolation from the others. My own favorite analogy for this is to think of the manner in which you attend to aspects of research design as similar to the way that you try to focus on the shifting patterns within a kaleidoscope. All of the same basic elements—fragments of colored glass—are present *all the time,* but the pattern of shapes and colors that comes into focus *at any one time* depends on how your shaking and twisting of the whole instrument position the contents. (Of course, to realize the full potential of this analogy, we must assume that you also have made the effort to gather the fragments of glass, determine which ones go into the mix, affix a lens, and actually construct the kaleidoscope.)

Chapters 2 through 6 address the process of conceptualizing and then establishing the coherence and fluidity of your inquiry through an exploration of the following key issues:

Engaging Problem and Purpose (Chapter 2)

This chapter works through the initial complexity of positioning yourself relative to a researchable problem and clarifying your intent in doing so.

Establishing Your Perspective (Chapter 3)

This chapter poses both guidelines and challenges tied to the construction of your intellectual orientation and moral stance as a researcher.

Constructing a Conceptual Context (Chapter 4)

This chapter suggests guidelines for constructing the conceptual context of your inquiry.

Forming Research Questions (Chapter 5)

This chapter addresses three major aspects of getting at and working with research questions: (a) moving toward your question, (b) justifying your question, and (c) going somewhere with your question.

Making Decisions About Traditions (Chapter 6)

This chapter presents strategies for determining when and how it matters to distinguish your approach to inquiry as a particular genre of field-based research (e.g., ethnography, grounded theory, phenomenology).

CHAPTER 2

ENGAGING PROBLEM AND PURPOSE

How do I transform what seems to be just an informed hunch or nagging concern into something that can drive a legitimate and purposeful inquiry? Where do I start? Where do I go with my ideas? Do I have a good reason for pursuing this? How do I reflect upon my developing sense of problem and purpose?

The clean, linear presentation of statements of problem or purpose that are typically found in scholarly chapters and journal articles provides a thin basis for understanding the initial mess and frustration of finding and fine-tuning a problem for your inquiry. More to the point, it inadvertently masks the play of problem finding in the preliminary phases of conceptualizing your research. This chapter directs attention to what it means to pose a researchable problem (or topic) and how you position that problem relative to the aims driving your inquiry.

Figure 2.1 provides a schematic description of the dynamic process encompassed by the phrase *engaging with a sense of problem*. As a means to conceptualize a strategy for holding on to and making sense of the ideas that are prompting your inquiry, it suggests a dynamic between *personal or immediate concerns* that drive an inquiry and *systematic considerations* that orient an inquiry. The former concerns represent a complex mix of direct experience, professional insight, intellectual orientation, intuition, emotional investment, and common sense. The latter considerations can be approached along more readily defined pathways that include:

- how and why you are choosing to position yourself relative to a particular problem or issue you have defined.
- why you are looking at issues in a particular way.
- when and how you are linking up your inquiry with the work and ideas of others.
- how you are developing and then justifying the questions that focus your research.
- how you are deciding on your approach to real-world observations and data gathering.

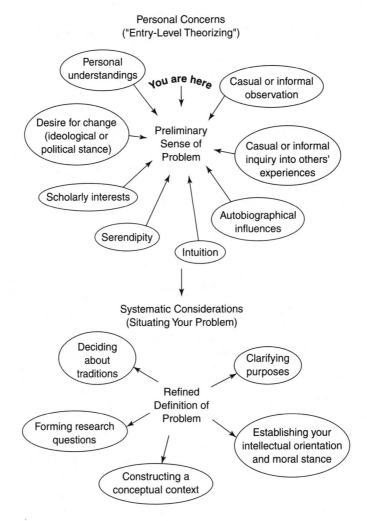

Figure 2.1
Engaging with a Sense of Problem from Personal Concerns to Systematic
Considerations

SHAPING A PRELIMINARY SENSE OF PROBLEM

Problem setting is the epitome of the research act. (Wolcott, 1992, p. 17)

Initially, the interplay and input of your direct experience and personal concerns
feed into the shaping of a sense of problem. At this stage, you're working at a level
of creative discomfort with any number of hunches, nagging concerns, and curiosi-

ties. Casual observations, informal inquiry into others' experiences, political commitments, scholarly or professional interests, intuition, and even serendipity are playing off each other to bring into question the way that you are viewing an issue or set of circumstances.

A sense of problem may take shape simply as a questioning of why something is one way and not another. Or, it may emerge as a hunch that something is missing in your understanding or interpretation of a situation. In any case, a sense of problem can, but need not, imply that something has gone wrong and must be fixed. As suggested in Chapter 1, qualitative studies typically do not aim at problem solution, but are exceptionally well suited to "problematizing" phenomena to reveal their complexity (Piantanida & Garman, 1999). Consider the following experience described by Patrice, in which a casual observation fed into a preliminary articulation of a problem for inquiry.

> *Sitting in a local restaurant as part of a recent off-site management meeting recently, I was distracted by a young man—presumably the father—cradling in his arms what looked to be a five-month-old infant. The baby had the attention of another adult who had positioned her body close to the man's side and was interacting with the baby by making gleeful, animated faces to which the infant clearly responded with pleasure.*
>
> *As this social interaction unfolded, the threesome attracted the attention of other bystanders, and the group grew. Within minutes, there were at least five adults in awe of this beautiful infant who knew how to charm the group with quick smiles, dancing eyes, and vocalizations that engaged everyone's attention. I interpreted all of this as healthy behavior that reflected the notions I held about what constitutes healthy development for infants. The social and emotional responses and interactions were as they should be and I assessed the infant to be delightfully "developmentally age-appropriate."*
>
> *The bothersome piece for me, however, was the contrast between the social situation I had just witnessed and informally assessed and the social situation of many of the infants for whom I am called upon to make similar, more formal assessments. When an infant is born into a context of poverty, what opportunities exist to facilitate what I know to be healthy social and emotional development? The families that I know who live in poverty do not have these same experiences; the restaurant scene would in many cases be an unfamiliar context for such interaction. Do I produce a valid assessment of infant social and emotional development when I apply my middle class constructs of infant well-being to infants and families who live in poverty?*

Patrice's firsthand knowledge and experience as an early intervention home visitor gave rise to her consideration that "we have a problem." In this case, her sense of problem emerged from the discomfort she felt when she observed infants and adults in "classic" social engagement situations (such as the restaurant episode) that leading child development experts would describe as "normal." Her discomfort stemmed, as she stated,

> . . . from knowing full well that not every baby has the opportunity for these experiences but has different experiences that may or may not promote optimal development. It is observing the emotion on a mother's face when a home visitor explains to the mother what will happen if her child "fails" a screening. Although I understand the intent and meaning of the home visitor, I also conclude that this mother has a history of negative emotions associated with failing, and a barrier between the home visitor and the mother has likely been erected.

Entry-Level Theorizing

Such observations and accompanying insights contributed to the play of ideas, emotions, and experiences that enabled Patrice to move toward an increasingly refined sense of problem. She engaged in a fluid and dialectic process of focusing her inquiry by alternately grasping and letting go of notions, interests, and questions like those described previously, situating herself relative to a problem that I equate to *entry-level theorizing* (Wolcott, 1995). Entry-level theorizing refers to "a thought-about position from which the researcher as inquirer feels drawn to an issue or problem and seeks to construct a firmer basis in both knowledge and understanding" (Wolcott, 1995, p. 186). Patrice subsequently conveyed her thought-about position in this way:

> Professionals in the field of infant development apply concepts of emotional health that have likely been created outside the context of poverty. If I adhere to the notion that what we know is socially constructed, then I question (a) the idea of what constitutes an emotionally healthy infant as determined by middle class researchers and practitioners, and (b) how we apply this definition to families who live under different circumstances, such as those families who live in poverty.
>
> If I am going to evaluate effectively and fairly the social and emotional development of infants in the context of poverty, I need to understand infant development from the perspectives of those who live in poverty. How do families who live in the context of poverty view infant well-being?

Taken together, the incorporation of personal experience and professional insight represented in these three excerpts from Patrice's preliminary journaling might take the practical form of a *researcher experience memo*, or *analytic memo* (Maxwell, 1996, building upon Mills, 1959). Making the effort to identify and explicitly take into account how your identity and experience are informing your sense of problem, and documenting that effort in a written memo, is a valuable and necessary strategy in the development of your inquiry. Keep in mind, as well, that this is not a one-time exercise. Although crucial at this early stage of problem finding, memos should resurface to inform, spur systematic reflection, and provide reality checks throughout the course of your inquiry (see "Mining Your Memos" later in this chapter).

A Word About Working Inductively . . . or Not

A careful look at Patrice's problem-finding efforts thus far also serves to steer us away from the misleading, but prevalent, characterization of qualitative inquiry as radically or exclusively inductive. Following Schwandt (1997) and Agar (1996), we can think of working *inductively* as moving from specific experiences and pieces of data to a more general explanation or formulation of an idea. Think in terms of putting together a jigsaw puzzle whose picture you do not yet know and which becomes apparent only as you collect and examine the pieces. Working *deductively*, in contrast, entails looking first to established theory—the big picture—to provide the definitions and hypotheses from which predictions can be derived and tested. In a sense, deductive researchers hope to find data to match, support, or validate a theory.

The issue of how you proceed with your inquiry is one of emphasis rather than either/or. Qualitative researchers characteristically operate with a "predisposition" (Glesne, 1999) toward a highly inductive approach to inquiry. If, however, you are tempted to insist that you are proceeding under the qualitative banner as a thoroughly inductive researcher, obliged to wait for a question to "emerge" from a setting and to do so without your own substantial input, stop and reconsider. The characteristic tentativeness of many qualitative researchers when pressed to explain what they are looking for should not be confused with some mysterious way in which they are waiting for a setting or a situation to spew forth a research question for them. "Probably the most serious misunderstanding (and biggest disappointment) about qualitative research," cautions Wolcott (1988), "is the realization that, just as with quantitative approaches, *we bring our questions with us* to the research setting" (p. 17).

In depicting the ebb and flow of inductive analysis in qualitative inquiry, Patton (2002) draws upon the useful notions of *fit* and *work* from Glaser and Strauss's (1967) original framing of grounded theory. Patton describes the play between an inductive mode, through which patterns and major dimensions of interest are revealed, and a more deductive emphasis on verification and clarification. "[W]hat is discovered may be verified by going back to the world under study and examining the extent to which the emergent analysis *fits* the phenomenon and *works* to explain what has been observed" (Patton, 2002, p. 67). It is not a linear or sequential process but a tacking back and forth between experience (including exposure to applicable theories) and reflection on experience.

It is common in discussions on this topic to apply the term *emergent design* to convey the responsiveness of a researcher's plans and strategies to changing circumstances. Like Schwandt (1997), I have come to view emergent design as "an unfortunate term for an important idea" (p. 34). As Schwandt explains,

If we use the strict sense of the word "emergent" (i.e., arising unexpectedly), it would be reasonable to say that the fieldworker does encounter emergent issues, emergent circumstances that call for a response, or both, and hence the plan for fieldwork ought to be flexible and adaptive. As a modifier for "design," however, the term "emergent" can suggest that the design itself arises unexpectedly or that the fieldworker has no design or plan at all at the outset of the study. (p. 35)

As illustrated in Patrice's preliminary efforts, some lines of inquiry and problem posing reflected the play of relevant theoretical or conceptual work done by others against the critical input of her own experience, intuition, and hunches. Other conceptualizations of Patrice's problem emerged or changed in response to her developing understanding of and exposure to events and ideas. As a qualitative researcher, you will likely start inductively. In the eventual development of questions and throughout your subsequent fieldwork, however, be prepared for an approach in which you are constantly and creatively moving between induction and deduction, or between discovery and verification (Patton, 2002; Rossman & Rallis, 1998; Schwandt, 1993; Strauss & Corbin, 1998).

Situating Your Problem

With her refined sense of problem, Patrice was now positioned to consider in more systematic fashion how she might link up with the work and ideas of others by addressing issues of purpose, theory, perspective, and method—in effect, *situating her problem*. This entails links with the ideas of others and consideration of the relationships among the key issues within one's design. These links, identified in the bottom half of Figure 2.1, will be discussed more thoroughly in Chapters 3, 4, 5, and 6.

When moving on from the personal and experiential emphases of entry-level theorizing, you continue to position yourself relative to a problem. However, as you engage with the systematic considerations of situating your problem, the generative flow of inquiry is from a refined definition of problem rather than toward a preliminary sense of problem. (Note the reversed direction of the arrows in Figure 2.1.) This is a decisive shift: You must now consider your inquiry as something that is constructed in relation to ideas, contexts, and purposes beyond the immediate scope of your direct experiences and observations. It is time to expand your notion of positioning to include how you identify, distinguish, and justify your research purposes; how and why you decide to look at the world and your particular problem in a certain way; how you link your thinking with the work and ideas of others; how you develop and justify your research question(s); and how you decide on strategies and methods for data collection, generation, and analysis.

Some words of caution: As I noted in the introduction to Part One, positioning yourself systematically demands that you consider all of these key issues at the same time and over a period of time. They are interconnected in such a way that the manner in which you respond to any one issue, taken in any order, affects how you respond to the others. This is another way of saying that, as a qualitative researcher, you work through complexity rather than around or in spite of it.

Finding a Point of Entry

The preceding words of caution still beg the question of where and how to find a point of entry into the multiple tasks of situating your problem and establishing systematic links among the various components of conceptualizing and designing your study. Taking that step is often a function of individual circumstances or serendipity—finding yourself drawn initially to the play of some intriguing concepts, for example, or perhaps feeling pressed to clarify your assumptions before you can proceed further. If there isn't a pull toward one component or another, experience suggests that clarifying one's intent or purpose is a logical and practical way to get on with situating your problem and, more broadly, your inquiry.

CLARIFYING PURPOSES

The task here is to make the connection between positioning yourself relative to a problem and clarifying your intent in doing so. This represents a subtle shift in emphasis, particularly if you regard the individual concerns and entry-level theorizing discussed in the previous section as tacit expressions of the personal or experiential purposes motivating your inquiry. It is important that you take into account your purposes at this personal level and acknowledge how they may be shaping your inquiry. At the same time you need to distinguish them from the more public and systematically generated statements of purpose that help to guide and justify your study, namely, research purposes and practical purposes (Maxwell, 1996).

Research Purposes and Practical Purposes

Consider the ways that Patrice could proceed depending on how she focuses the purpose of her inquiry. She might describe her aims in terms of understanding something or gaining insight into what is going on in a setting—that is, a *research* purpose (Maxwell, 1996). For example: "The purpose of this study is to understand the experience of families who participate in early intervention programs," or "The purpose of this study is to explore infant well-being as described by families who are impacted by poverty." Either of these purposes can be addressed directly by an empirical field study.[1]

Contrast this researchable aim with a statement of purpose focused on accomplishing, changing, or evaluating something—that is, a *practical* purpose (Maxwell, 1996). For example: "The purpose of this study is to generate program changes that will improve the experiences of families impacted by poverty," or "The purpose of

---

[1] The word *empirical* has been widely misused to refer only to quantified data. Used correctly, as Metz (2000) reminds us, it refers to "information that has been gathered in any systematic way about the world around us as it is available through experience rather than through mere deduction" (p. 68). Qualitative data, in Metz's view and according to the presentation of ideas in this text, are "profoundly empirical."

this study is to identify ways that home-visiting human service providers can more effectively partner with families as a way to promote healthy infant development." Neither of these purposes can be directly addressed by empirical research even though each reflects a valuable aim. Patrice acknowledged both emphases within her efforts early on and described her concern for maintaining the "authenticity" of her research:

> It seems that what I want to do is some sort of "transformative" research . . . but I'm not sure I want to claim that because I would have to go into my site assuming, for example, that the relationships [between the early intervention service providers and the families] serve to perpetuate poverty. However, I think I can go in saying, "If that, then this," meaning, "If I see behaviors and interactions that perpetuate poverty, then I will take an approach that could lead to some sort of action." My caution remains, however, that if I go into a site with an agenda [to change the situation], my research won't be authentic.

By maintaining the distinction between her research purposes and practical purposes, Patrice can establish as a legitimate part of her design a discussion of how her inquiry may (and perhaps should) create opportunities for social action, change, or advocacy (Marshall & Rossman, 1999). This complementary discussion of practical aims would flow from (but certainly not substitute for) her primary focus on research purposes that can feed directly into the framing of questions answerable by an empirical study. The key point here: Make sure that it is your research that prompts any recommendations for change, rather than the intended recommendations framing the research (Hess, 1999). (Chapter 3 will return to this issue in the context of where and how you make known your perspective as a researcher.)

Distinguishing Focus and Locus

The task of homing in on research purposes directs attention as well to the important distinction between the focus and locus of one's inquiry. I was first alerted to the significance of this distinction during my own graduate studies in anthropology and education when I encountered these cautionary words from Clifford Geertz: "The locus of study is not the object of study. Anthropologists don't study villages (tribes, towns, neighborhoods . . .); they study *in* villages" (Geertz, 1973, p. 22). In other words, when considering how to convey the purposes of your research, do not confuse where you are looking (or what you are looking at) with what you are looking for.

Why is this so important? It is easy to become captivated by what you perceive to be the intrinsic value or appeal of a particular situation, such as a stellar classroom teacher who weaves her pedagogical magic with a group of students or an exciting cross-cultural teacher exchange program. Such an opportunity, if construed to be the focus of inquiry, may set you up to provide an engaging, descriptive, even affirming (pat-on-the-back) account. However, it falls short of identifying a conceptual issue or concern that effectively orients you to attend (or not to attend) to certain things in the conduct of your research. Keep yourself appropriately focused by continuing to revisit these questions: "What's at issue here? What's going to convey the broader conceptual significance of this study?"

The focus of Patrice's study was not the Early Head Start program per se; rather, the Early Head Start program was the context in which she embedded her concern for how people in different socioeconomic and cultural circumstances perceive infant well-being. Your study's *focus,* as ultimately reflected in your statement of research purpose, should direct attention to conceptual concerns. Your study's *locus* is where you locate these concerns, bounding them in time and circumstance.

An underlying risk linked with emphasizing locus over focus in your research purpose is finding yourself on the shaky ground of what Geertz (in building his earlier claim) termed the "heaven in a grain of sand" model for justifying the significance of one's work (1973, p. 21). In Patrice's case, it would be like saying, "The particular early intervention program I am studying *is* early intervention in America writ small." If particular, localized studies—the grist of qualitative research—were actually dependent for their greater relevance upon this type of premise, then we would indeed be on shaky ground. *Typicality* is not part of the bread-and-butter mix of qualitative inquiry, and we need to take care that our statements of research purpose do not imply that it is. Remember that your focus, the conceptual seed of your study's significance, is what lies *in* your particular village.

Purposes and Going Qualitative

Another important connection in the design process is the compatibility of your purposes (personal, research, and practical) and your reasons for pursuing a qualitative approach. Historically, qualitative researchers have claimed the following as major purposes for inquiry:

- **Descriptive aims** to document and describe what is happening in a setting, event, or set of circumstances;
- **Interpretive aims** to investigate important categories of meaning; to understand how the particular context in which participants act influences their behavior and actions; or to uncover and/or generate questions or hypotheses for further research; and
- **Explanatory or theoretical aims** to identify and analyze patterns, including unanticipated influences, related to what is happening; and to identify plausible relationships shaping what is happening (Erickson, 1986; Marshall & Rossman, 1999; Maxwell, 1992).

In the past decade or so, studies grounded in critical, postmodern, or feminist assumptions have extended consideration of research purposes to include an emphasis on action, advocacy, or empowerment. Brantlinger (1999) and Marshall and

Rossman (1999) exemplify a substantial body of scholars who account for this and strongly promote the following category:

- **Emancipatory aims**   to raise awareness and create opportunities to engage in social action and seek social justice.

Patrice's research purposes appear to emphasize the interpretive (addressing how participants give meaning to the concept of infant well-being) and the descriptive (documenting the experiences of participants in the program). The practical purpose embedded within her research (to somehow improve the experience of families served by the program), especially when considered in light of the personal concerns motivating her inquiry, suggests an implicit emancipatory emphasis.

These categories, while helpful to Patrice for clarifying the compatibility of her aims with an intended ethnographic approach (see Chapter 6), should not be construed as a way to measure her decision to "go qualitative" against some minimum requirements or optimum combination of stated (and unstated) purposes. (Imagine going to your thesis advisor to defend your qualitative approach by claiming, "My proposed study will be 50% descriptive, 35% interpretive, and 15% emancipatory!") Instead, think of these categories less as a standard and more as one of a number of strategies for ensuring that the various elements of your research design inform, and are consistent with, each other.

It is also important to recognize that your purposes are influenced by the way you look at the world, interpret what you see, and decide which things you see are valid and important to document. In this respect, your orchestration of connections within the design process continues to work you simultaneously through greater complexity and toward finer focus. This is the work of positioning yourself relative to a problem and clarifying your intent in doing so, as discussed in this chapter. It also entails building an orientation and a context for your inquiry, in terms of which your inquiry, and your reasons and strategies for pursuing it, make sense. Constructing an intellectual orientation and moral stance is the focus of Chapter 3. Chapter 4 addresses the construction of a conceptual context for your inquiry.

MINING YOUR MEMOS

Early on in this chapter I highlighted Maxwell's (1996) notion of analytic memos as an invaluable means for you to reflect upon and develop ideas around your topic of inquiry. Before closing out this discussion of problem and purpose I want to return to some practical considerations around the use of memos as a tool for conceptualizing your inquiry.

Like Maxwell, my students and I have found that "memos do for ideas what fieldnotes and transcripts do for perception: they convert thought into a form that allows examination and further manipulation" (Maxwell, 1996, p. 12). The "examination and further manipulation" piece is the key consideration. Memos are eminently practical as a source of "data" for your developing sense of problem and direction for inquiry.

Initially, you generate the *stuff* of memos. That is, as illustrated in Patrice's earlier reflections, you reflect in writing on a personal experience or an insightful reading, or you pour out a stream of consciousness response to a colleague's comment. As you write, you are not usually grasping the significance and place of this or that idea in the bigger scheme of things. You are getting it down, sensing perhaps its potential as a way to help you come to terms with your problem or topic. You then revisit your memos: building connections within and between some of them, and wondering what in the world you were thinking when you wrote others. But you hold on to and file all of them.

Ultimately, as with fieldnotes and interview transcripts, you face the practical necessity of reducing the complexity and volume of lived experience and spur-of-the-moment ideas into something you can grasp. Reexamined *out* of the moment and in the context of additional "data," once familiar and taken-for-granted ideas captured in your memos can take on new significance. Contradictions or connections in your thinking may start to become apparent: "Look at this: all this time I've been claiming that *this* is the focus of my inquiry. So why have so many of my reflections directed attention to *that*? I need to rethink this." "Aha! There, within those two previously unconnected phrases, I can begin to see a way to state my purpose."

Oftentimes, such insights are garnered through the sharing of your written memos with others. In my research classes I regularly encourage such sharing, or "mining" of memos, but always predicate it upon the following caution: "[T]hinking of memos primarily as a means of communicating to *other* people will inevitably interfere with the kind of reflective writing that you need to do to make memos most useful to you" (Maxwell, 1996, p. 12). Memos are cumulative and meant to be personally useful; they should reflect *thinking in progress* rather than polished ideas intended for others. Make them your own.

SUMMARY

The process of *engaging with a sense of problem* encompasses the dynamic interplay between personal or immediate concerns that drive an inquiry and systematic considerations that orient an inquiry. This chapter provided a point of entry into this complex process by addressing the preliminary task of positioning yourself relative to a researchable problem. At this level of engagement, you as inquirer try to construct a basis of knowledge and understanding, a thought-about position from which you can develop a more refined definition of problem.

With that definition in hand, you are positioned to consider in more systematic fashion how your inquiry makes sense in relation to ideas, contexts, and purposes beyond the immediate scope of your direct and personal experiences. *Situating your problem* refers to how you go about linking up with the work and ideas of others by addressing issues of purpose, theory, perspective, and method. This chapter addressed the first of these concerns, purpose, by highlighting key distinctions (a) between research purposes and practical purposes, (b) between the focus and locus of one's inquiry, and (c) among the descriptive, interpretive, theoretical, and emancipatory aims that, in varying levels of emphasis, can characterize a qualitative approach.

Determination of how you proceed with your inquiry is generally a matter of emphasis rather than deciding on one approach or perspective to the exclusion of another. This is evident in the play of ideas that inform the aims of your inquiry and will become even more apparent as we consider the identity-clarifying and context-building issues explored in Chapters 3 and 4.

CHAPTER 3

ESTABLISHING YOUR PERSPECTIVE

What perspective, or intellectual orientation, am I bringing to this research? Why is that important? What does it mean to be a social inquirer, not only in intellectual and ideological terms but also in a moral sense? Where and how is my perspective made apparent in my work?

This chapter directs attention to the following interrelated tasks:

- constructing an intellectual orientation or *intellectual identity* (Lareau, 1989), an explicit articulation of basic premises that influence the stance from which and the lens through which you view the world
- developing a sense of what it means to be a social inquirer in a moral sense, a clarification of the basis for your decisions about how to be *with* study participants and respond to controversies and ethical dilemmas in your relationships with others involved in your inquiry

CONSTRUCTING AN INTELLECTUAL ORIENTATION

All research is informed by basic beliefs or premises about the world and how it should be understood and studied. Taken together, these beliefs contribute to one's worldview, frame of reference, or *paradigm*. [1] The beliefs are basic in the sense that they can never be established in terms of their ultimate truthfulness. Rather, they must be accepted simply on faith and the persuasiveness and utility of their arguments (Guba & Lincoln, 1994; Lincoln & Guba, 2000; Schwandt, 1997).

In practical terms, paradigms, sometimes called *inquiry paradigms,* are important to you as a researcher because they define how you view the world and provide a basis for deciding which of the things you see are legitimate and important to document. Positioning yourself relative to a paradigm entails:

- defining a stance for yourself by committing to a basic set of beliefs.
- considering the lens through which you will filter these beliefs.
- articulating how these first two processes might lead you to identify with a particular way of viewing the world and your inquiry.

---

[1] With Rossman and Rallis (1998) and others, I believe that the term *paradigm* has been "overworked, overused, and trivialized" (p. 55). But also like them, I have found it useful as a term that students can hold on to (at least initially) to help them position their work and ideas within a potentially confusing array of claims and constructs.

Your Stance: Committing to a Basic Set of Beliefs

Patrice's decision to inquire into the experiences of families impacted by poverty turned, in large part, on the personal concerns, practical aims, and research purposes described in the previous chapter. Her decision to look at these experiences in a particular way turned, ultimately, on her response to some fundamental philosophical questions that all researchers must address at one point or another:

- What can I assume about "how things really are" in a setting?
- How do I learn about something?
- If someone were to ask me, "How do you know that?," what is acceptable evidence that whatever it is I claim to know is accurate?

Breaking these questions down still further, you can think of your intellectual identity-building efforts in terms of the following issues (adapted from Creswell, 1998; Guba & Lincoln, 1988, 1994; Lincoln & Guba, 2000; Rossman & Rallis, 1998).

The Ontological Issue

What is the nature of reality and what can be known about it? This refers to what Patrice might assume about "how things really are" in the setting she is investigating. For Patrice, following a premise common to qualitative studies, "how things really are" was a function of multiple perspectives, including those of the researcher, those of individuals being investigated, and those of the readers who would interpret the completed study (Creswell, 1998). As she stated:

> The "multiple nature of reality" issue points to my position that truth and reality are constructed by individuals within various social contexts; there is no universal, objective truth. In my research I expect this to be evident in perceptions of infant well-being. My notion of infant well-being has been constructed from my experiences and shaped in the context of my middle class background. I believe that individuals who grow up in poverty, become parents, and raise children in the context of poverty will have different perspectives on infant well-being. I do not believe there can be an objective theory that states infant well-being looks like this, universally, across all settings, contexts, and cultures.

The Epistemological Issue

How do we come to "know" the world? What is the relationship between the researcher and what can be researched? This refers to the posture Patrice might assume relative to the participants in her study and is directly dependent on her belief, described previously, that "how things are" is a function of multiple perspectives. Given this understanding, it is not only appropriate but also necessary for Patrice to actively observe or engage in the lives of those whose perspectives she is seeking to understand. This is contrary to a stance of objective detachment between the researcher's influence and the people and events being studied—a stance that might follow from assuming, for example, that there is a single "true" perspective on infant well-being. Patrice's conceptions of the relationship between researcher and researched played off fundamental considerations of what could and could not be known solely from her own perspective:

> *I have felt comfortable in social and economic settings similar to that of my own childhood, and I find it easy to relate to families who have a similar interaction style and who share goals and priorities for their children similar to my own. It is the feeling of "disconnect," however, that intrigues me about my relationships with families who live in circumstances different from my own, and that emphasizes the need for me to engage more fully in their reality in order to understand their perspectives. What are the priorities of a family who is perpetually homeless when that family's goals do not seem to include housing? My need to address such questions compels me to connect directly with the lives and experiences of these families.*

The Methodological Issue

How does the researcher go about inquiring into whatever he or she believes can be researched? This refers to how Patrice might conceptualize the entire research process, an issue that feeds directly from the distinctions she was making about the nature of reality and what can be known about the world. At this point she establishes the philosophical cornerstone for all her subsequent decisions about how to proceed, as she begins to figure out that not just *any* methodology is appropriate for her inquiry.

This is a good opportunity to clarify that I am discussing *methodology* as distinct from *method*. Methodology refers to the theory and analysis of how inquiry does or should proceed (Metz, 2000). It entails careful examination of the issues, principles, and procedures associated with a particular approach to inquiry, say ethnography, that in turn guide the use of particular methods (Schwandt, 1997, 2000). *Method* commonly denotes a specific procedure, tool, or technique used by the researcher to generate and analyze data—the means supporting the theory of where you want to go with your inquiry. For example, long interviews, augmented with researcher self-reflection, are a method often associated with phenomenological studies (see Chapter 6 for further clarification of these distinctions).

In Patrice's case, a reality built upon multiple perspectives and investigated by a researcher immersed in the lives of the researched suggested a methodology characterized by:

- a letting go of control of possible confounding variables (for example, who in the setting is willing to talk to her about particular issues);
- an emphasis on describing in detail the context in which people's perspectives are being shaped and shared;
- the need to work with particulars (details) before general explanations (the big picture); and
- an openness to the continual refinement of questions based on knowledge gained in the field.

Note once again that the way Patrice responded to the methodological issue was delimited by the manner in which she responded to the ontological and epistemological issues. The way she was making sense of, and making a case for, her developing perspective as an inquirer was consistent across all three categories of belief.

Your Lens: Thinking About Your View of the Social World

Assumptions are also at work to influence the particular way you look at society and social phenomena. Once again, making these assumptions explicit is important for understanding, and making clear to others, why you attend to some things but not to others in the conduct of your inquiry. A fundamental issue is whether you tend to view the social world with greater measures of (a) satisfaction with how things are or (b) concern about how things should change. It is likely that elements of each are at play, in varying amounts, in whatever you do. What matters in the context of your inquiry is the extent to which you allow your perspective to play out, for example, in the way you distinguish and portray your purposes (see Chapters 2 and 7) or in the way you choose to involve participants in your study (see Chapter 7).

The predominant orientation in social science, as Rossman and Rallis (1998) note, has been to focus on the cohesiveness and functionality of the status quo. There is a comforting rationality and predictability to this perspective, an attitude that things and people make sense, work together, and function to address certain needs. Researchers with this mind-set engage in the business of sense making and generating knowledge about what makes the world go round and what might make it go round even better.

In contrast, the emphasis that characterizes the work of an increasing number of researchers reflects an underlying (but presumably conscious) assumption "that things are not right as they are or, most certainly, are not as good as they might be" (Wolcott, 1992, p. 15). Change directed at improvement defines the agenda of such inquiry. This calls for the inquirer to establish in a sensitive and credible manner the distinction between compelling interest in an issue and heartfelt advocacy for a cause (Rossman & Rallis, 1998).

Patrice embodied an effective and workable balance of these orientations. Her personal aim to become "a more effective help giver" was a persistent refrain in her design efforts, as was her extended practical aim of helping other service providers be more effective with the families they served. The operative assumption was that she could work with and make sense of how things were and then perhaps make them better. At the same time, she expressed her underlying sense that something was clearly wrong in the fact that privileged people (including herself) presumed to interact with and serve a particular population without giving much thought to whether they really understood its members' lives and perspectives. That was an unacceptable state of affairs that should be changed and presumably could be changed to some degree by her research.

In the process of composing your inquiry, you need to consider how your responses to the issues discussed thus far might lead you to identify with a perspective that orients your beliefs and assumptions even more specifically. This is a crucial aspect of situating your inquiry: You need to connect what you are looking at (the problem), and why (your purposes), with a particular way of knowing and looking (your paradigm or worldview). The following section provides some possibilities for you to explore.

Connecting with a Paradigm: Some Key Examples

In this section I address three paradigms—interpretive, critical, and ecological—the differences between which seem to have significant implications for the conduct of qualitative inquiry. Although relying on several categories suggested by LeCompte and Schensul (1999), my selection of these particular paradigms is a judgment call; I tend to regard them as *situated* (connected to other paradigms) and *contested* (subject to debate even among their proponents). I certainly have not tried to exhaust all possibilities around the issue of paradigms (there are more out there), but I do hope to suggest through these examples how commitment to a particular frame of reference steers you in the direction of a particular kind of inquiry. Accordingly, my comments should be understood as a modest reconnaissance of the philosophical or ideological terrain in which you might locate and legitimize your research perspective rather than as a (very incomplete) shopping list from which you simply choose an appealing worldview.

The following categorizations and definitions draw heavily upon the ideas generated by Brantlinger (1999), Guba and Lincoln (1994), Kincheloe and McLaren (1994, 2000), LeCompte and Schensul (1999), Lincoln and Guba (2000), Rossman and Rallis (1998), and Schwandt (1994, 2000). For further clarification of these and related paradigms I encourage you to consult these sources.

The Interpretive Paradigm

Even if you are relatively new to the field of qualitative inquiry, you have likely encountered the terms *interpretivist, constructivist, naturalistic, phenomenological,* and *hermeneutical,* among other variants. Each has its proponents who argue for their term's unique meaning: sociologists, educators, and psychologists advocating for constructivism; philosophers arguing for phenomenology; and anthropologists touting interpretivism. Just as often, these terms are used interchangeably to denote similar notions or shared understandings. Following LeCompte and Schensul (1999), I will use the term *interpretive* (or *interpretivist*) as a general descriptor for what might best be regarded as "a loosely coupled family of methodological and philosophical persuasions" (Schwandt, 1994, p. 118).

Proponents of this family of persuasions share the belief that "what people know and believe to be true about the world is constructed—or made up—as people interact with one another over time in specific social settings" (LeCompte & Schensul, 1999, p. 48). A frequently cited phrase associated with this notion is the "social construction of reality" (Berger & Luckmann, 1967). As an interpretivist researcher, your aim is to understand this complex and constructed reality from the point of view of those who live in it. Necessarily, then, you are focused on particular people, in particular places, at particular times—situating people's meanings and constructs within and amid specific social, political, cultural, economic, ethnic, and other contextual factors.

Interpretivists operate from the belief that all constructs are equally important and valid. Remember, for example, Patrice's assumption regarding the need to attend to multiple perspectives. This belief presents challenging implications, especially when you consider that the task of interpretation is to construct a "reading" of these multiple meanings and voices—in effect, offering your "own construction of other people's constructions of what they . . . are up to" (Geertz, 1973, p. 9). Generating and synthesizing these multi-voiced and varied constructions requires that you engage at some level in the lives of those around whom your inquiry is focused; it is through direct interaction with their perspectives and behaviors that you focus and refine your interpretations.

Participation or interaction of this sort does not imply a change-oriented posture on the part of the inquirer. At the same time, you might be hard pressed as a social science researcher nowadays to avoid the expectation that your inquiry serve in some way as a vehicle for reform. How you position yourself in this regard turns on the nature and explicitness of your intentions. If and when you do commit to function as an advocate or to investigate possibilities for change in a situation, then you begin to connect your inquiry to a critical paradigm.

The Critical Paradigm

A *critical* approach is consistent with the view that researchers should engage in inquiry with the expectation that their work will be instrumental in bringing about change.[2] Advocacy and activism are the key concepts, calling for the researcher to speak *for* some (oppressed or exploited) person or group and *from* a particular (ideological or political) position, rather than simply speak *to* an audience *about* a group or phenomena of interest (Appadurai, 1988). To be critical is to ask questions that probe at potentially negative effects, such as "Whose interests are being served?" and "Whose interests are likely to be ignored?" (Bushnell, 2001; Magolda, 2000). Anthropologist Michael Agar (1996) offers a helpful summary in his assessment of critical ethnography:

> Underneath all the different interpretations of the term *critical* lies a common thread—you look at local context and meaning, just like we always have, but then you ask, *why* are things this way? What power, what interests, wrap this local world so tight that it feels like the natural order of things to its inhabitants? Are those inhabitants even aware of those interests, aware that they have alternatives? And then—the critical move that blows the old scientific attitude right off the map— maybe *I*, the ethnographer, should show them choices they don't even know they have. Maybe I should shift from researcher to political activist. (p. 26)

In other words, critical inquirers add to the interpretivist's task—attending to and interpreting a perspective—the responsibility of helping others, including those in the immediate setting, attend to and act upon a perspective. This suggests an approach that may be just as participatory but is clearly more confrontational and value-mediated than that of interpretivists. It moves researchers beyond a concern for describing what *is* and pushes them and others toward the question of what *could be*.

---

[2] A number of leading scholars use the term *critical theory* as a blanket term to denote a set of several alternative paradigms. Guba and Lincoln (1994; Lincoln & Guba, 2000), for example, include neo-Marxism, feminism, materialism, and participatory inquiry within this set. They further suggest that the critical paradigm might productively be divided into three subcategories: poststructuralism, postmodernism, and a blending of these two. The common element of all these categories, they assert, is the *value-mediated* nature of the inquiry.

A basic premise of the critical paradigm is that the researcher, cast in the role of instigator and facilitator, understands a priori what changes are needed in a situation; the task of understanding is "cast in a prejudgmental framework" (Wolcott, 1999, p. 181; see also Lincoln & Guba, 2000). The values of the researcher inevitably influence the inquiry as he or she foregrounds the judgment call that an injustice is holding back someone from something better. This places the particular demand upon researchers to make explicit how their own class status, ethnic or gender orientation, and power relationships relative to research participants affect what is investigated and how data are interpreted. Patrice traced her own growing intrigue with a critical lens in this excerpt from an early draft of her research design:

> I began to think critically about my own position, including the position I hold with my employment—a middle class service provider and administrator of services provided to families who often (but not exclusively) live in poverty. Why do I often feel more comfortable providing service to those who have less than I have, rather than to those who have more? Does my appreciation of class diversity really point to my relief at being middle class? In a selfish way, does it help me to be grateful for what I have—a decent house, access to medical care, and a full pantry?
>
> Is there an ideological something (more than just paying lip service to "no more taxes") about who we are as Americans—our sociopolitical constitution—that prevents us from accepting Big Government to support an equalization of opportunity, to create social justice for all? As I reflected on the nature of our sociopolitical system, I began to wonder if our social service agencies unknowingly perpetuate inequitable relationships of class and power between providers and recipients of services.

Patrice's comments, while not definitively locating her in the critical arena, suggest two levels of concern that distinguish critical inquirers. On the one hand is the thick brush stroke emphasis on investigating the ways in which gender, class, culture, ethnicity, and power intersect to shape inequities—the characteristic aim of critique and transformation (Guba & Lincoln, 1994). Patrice's comments suggest that she is seeking "not merely to understand, but to understand *what is wrong,* and to link the problem to some greater wrong operating at some grander scale" (Wolcott, 1999, p. 181).

On the other hand is the finer focus on researchers themselves taking stock of who they are and from where they come. This latter effort entails researchers' awareness of differences between themselves and research participants, including how these perceived differences may influence both the flow of communication in the field setting and the later use of research results.

A Key Variation on the Critical Theme: Feminist Ideologies

Feminist ideology (or theory or epistemology, depending on whom you read) places gender front and center in its focus on oppressive social structures and the means to challenge and change them. It is grounded in a moral premise that assumes that the inequitable treatment of men and women is unjust. Women are viewed as oppressed by men through long-standing historical structures that support and legitimate oppression (Farganis, 1994). An underlying premise of feminist work, however, is that gender oppression is not experienced in isolation from considerations of race, class, culture, ethnicity, and other identities (Maguire, 1996).

Feminist researchers question the role that power and relationship play not only at the societal level but also at the personal level between researcher and researched. They seek to establish collaborative and nonexploitative relationships through the research process and reflect upon how those relationships affect the story being told. This corresponds to an overall feminist questioning about ideas of objectivity and neutrality and a rejection of the "distancing" that traditional social science upholds as the only way to observe fairly. Feminists' emphasis upon engagement with study participants reflects a heightened awareness of *intersubjectivity,* the idea "that whatever is created through the research is different because two or more people have interacted to build new meaning" (Glesne, 1999, p. 13).

Like the broad category of critical theory, there is no single feminist epistemology, but rather a number of distinct strands (e.g., feminist standpoint theories, feminist postmodernism, feminist empiricism). Patton (2002) suggests that critical theory and feminist inquiry both fall under the category of *orientational qualitative inquiry.* By this Patton means inquiry that begins with an explicit theoretical or ideological perspective that determines the study's conceptual framework and interpretation of findings. For example, a study undertaken from a feminist perspective would presume the importance of gender in human relationships and orient the study accordingly.

The Ecological Paradigm

Like the critical approach, the *ecological* paradigm builds upon the basic notion that individuals are embedded in and affected by a social context that influences their behaviors. Beyond this premise there are more points of contrast than of similarity between the two paradigms. Ecologically oriented researchers do not necessarily draw upon concepts of class, power, and equity to guide their inquiry, and unlike critical theorists, they have few preconceived notions about which structures or influences are most important.

The ecological paradigm's extensive history, particularly in ethnographic research, stems from the sociological work of Emile Durkheim and the even earlier anthropological work of scholars such as Bronislaw Malinowski and A. R. Radcliffe Brown. This perspective considers social systems in their entirety and aims to identify relationships across levels and structures (e.g., family groups, peer networks, school settings, community, the wider society) in local situations. For researchers using this approach, knowing "how things really are" is a matter of understanding the continuous accommodations among individuals, institutions, and the human and physical environment (Poggie, DeWalt, & Dressler, 1992); the emphasis is on understanding adaptation rather than generating shared meanings or instigating transformation.

The role of the researcher in this type of research tends neither to be informed by the inquirer's personal experience in interaction with study participants (as in an interpretivist or critical approach) nor to be transformative or deliberately educative (as in a critical approach). Ecologically minded researchers instead proceed with a definitive and relatively detached (from study participants) grasp upon the tasks of description and analysis aimed at identifying those contextual factors with the greatest influence on individual or institutional behaviors. Change, if and when it comes, is something that is best considered as being introduced in all levels and structures simultaneously, as befits a systemic perspective.

Clarifying Your Stance

My use of the phrase "*connecting* with a paradigm" rather than claiming or adopting a paradigm is deliberate; the notion is rarely so definitive as to expect that you can simply transfer a frame of reference unchanged from one research context to another. Most researchers do tend to emphasize their connection with one or another paradigm, while some situate their inquiry within a synthesis of two or more paradigms.

Patrice's approach, for example, represents something of a *paradigmatic synthesis* (LeCompte & Schensul, 1999) through which she is likely to connect with useful elements from at least two identifiable perspectives. Her emphasis on the social construction of individual and shared meanings, and her recognition of the influence of contextual factors on this process, suggests that she might benefit from interpretivist guidelines. She stops short of identifying a direction of change from the start, but the explicitness with which she has begun to address her own class status and power relationships relative to study participants suggests that she also may be positioning herself, at least in part, as a critical inquirer.[3]

Regardless of the connections you make, the frame of reference from which you view your inquiry represents a conscious choice that informs and extends your research aims, including how, and by whom, your data are interpreted and put to use (LeCompte & Schensul, 1999; Schwandt, 1993). As such, it is important to consider not only which paradigmatic elements inform your inquiry but how consistent they are with the other components of your research design. Do the connections among problem, purpose, and paradigm make sense? How do these connections strengthen the coherence and focus of your proposed research? Working through these questions to clarify the logic and aims of your paradigmatic stance contributes directly to how you go about constructing the conceptual context (Chapter 4) and guiding questions (Chapter 5) for your inquiry, as well as how you choose among methodological options (Chapter 6).

THE MORAL DIMENSIONS OF BEING A RESEARCHER

Thus far we have focused your identity-building efforts on how you believe the world should be understood and studied, on the one hand, and assumptions that influence the particular way you look at society and social phenomena, on the other.

---

[3] At the time of this writing, Patrice was well into her fieldwork, having established an especially open and supportive relationship with one of the Early Head Start mothers in her study. Her growing awareness of the "silenced voice" of this woman within the context of an oppressive, male-dominated household was positioning Patrice, at least tentatively, to question the direction that a feminist epistemological stance might take her inquiry.

Now it is time to ask: What does it mean to be a social inquirer, not only in intellectual and ideological terms but also in a moral sense? How do you unite the analytical with the ethical?

Fieldwork requires researchers to confront controversies, encouraging (or more often compelling) them to make decisions that draw upon values, ethical codes, professional standards, intuition, and feelings, and to ask themselves,

- "Is what I am doing a 'right' or 'good' thing to do?"
- "How shall I *be* toward these people [study participants]?"
- "Would I want others to be this way toward me?"
- "Do I regard my social interaction with study participants only as a means to an end? If not, how do I respond to conflicts of interest in the overlapping of my roles and relationships?"

For purposes of illustration, I am leaping ahead to an excerpt from Patrice's preliminary fieldwork that highlights a moment of unanticipated vulnerability and frustration she had to confront. Her comments refer to an interaction in the home of one of her key study participants, designated as "P." The interaction involved P's two-year-old daughter and, in particular, Patrice's observation in a moment of play that this little girl's speech development might be delayed. Patrice later reflected on the dilemma she faced:

> In this situation, just what are the considerations? Because I have highly specialized knowledge in infant and toddler development, should I share my observations with others around me? The family? The Early Head Start home visitor? To what extent am I really joining the circle of care around this child? If I fully join the circle of care, what influence does this have on research matters? Should I simply observe and see how long it takes for the home visitor to make a referral? If I share my observations, will I look like a know-it-all who is interfering and undermining the credibility of the Early Head Start Program?
> . . . And why did I not recognize this as an ethical issue right away?

Patrice later unpacked these questions in her fieldwork journal:

> I just don't know what to do or how to help. It is frustrating for me to be in the midst of this complex social system [of Early Head Start families and home visitors] and feel like I should be helping somehow to make things better and then reminding myself that I am there to observe and learn, not in the helping role. On the other hand, I have a professional conscience that sits on my shoulder that makes me feel like I should be helping, but I am so confused and overwhelmed by all of the factors that I wouldn't even know where to begin. So I guess I have to be satisfied that my presence alone helps P [the mother] and the kids, at least, because I can help P by getting her places and giving her another woman to talk to. And maybe I am a positive influence on the kids, able to provide a little bit of nurturing in the midst of a chaotic home environment.

"Ethical dilemmas that admit of no comfortable outcome but must be lived are experiences that researchers need to know about," notes de Laine (2000, p. 4). Patrice's dilemma, anticipated or not, serves as a reminder that a moral choice must be made that differentiates between being a disinterested and detached researcher or one who is genuinely interested in being involved with others and their needs (Schwandt, 1995). These two perspectives may express extremes, but they do help to set parameters for determining the degree to which you want or need to be involved during fieldwork in social, ethical, and emotional terms.

Denzin (1997) discusses two such ethical models in relation to fieldwork in the social sciences. The *traditional ethical model,* of which Denzin is critical, operates from the assumption that solutions can be made for ethical problems and dilemmas on rational, objective grounds; emotions and intuition are secondary. The research norm of *informed consent,* according to which participants learn of the researcher's role and purpose prior to fieldwork, is illustrative of this approach. The *feminist communitarian ethical model,* in contrast, assumes personally involved, self-reflexive researchers who hold themselves personally responsible for the political and ethical consequences of their actions. Such researchers "are expected to build collaborative, reciprocal, trusting, and friendly relations with those studied and value the connectedness that forms between them and others" (de Laine, 2000, p. 28).

Keep in mind that it is not an either/or proposition. Each type of problem requires a different approach, and some problems and dilemmas defy solutions. Chapter 8's discussion of ethical considerations in anticipation of fieldwork details several key dimensions of your role as a moral decision maker.

WHERE AND HOW DO YOU MAKE YOUR PERSPECTIVE KNOWN?

Where do you make your perspective known? Everywhere, and nowhere in particular. Despite the fact that my students rank this response right up there with the frustratingly prevalent "It depends," my words are intended to convey the pervasive but subtle play of your perspective in your inquiry. Having just worked your way through this chapter devoted to the process of clarifying your intellectual and moral positioning, you may well be questioning: "'*Subtle*'? What about all this effort I just put into making explicit my fundamental beliefs and values? Surely there's a place and a reason to showcase all that I've uncovered about my epistemological stance, worldview, and all that." Actually, no, at least not in the sense of exposing your intellectual and moral self for its own sake or simply to show others what you are made of; but neither does this mean that you should conceal your perspective and political views.

You give voice to your perspective in discussing how you engage with a preliminary sense of problem and purpose (Chapter 2) and how you portray your involvement with study participants (Chapter 7). You reveal it in the way you choose to define key concepts supporting the logic and coherence of your inquiry (Chapter 4) and in the degree and types of information you share with study participants (Chapter 8). Your perspective finds expression in terms of how you address assumptions within your research questions (Chapter 5) and in your decision to pursue a more or less participatory approach to research (Chapter 6). In short, your intellectual, ideological, or moral stance should inform all aspects of your conceptualization in the sense of being essential to your argument and justifications. It should speak *to* your developing inquiry rather than speak about itself in the form of "political polemic or irrelevant self-display" (Maxwell, 1996, p. 115) or simply a "decorative flourish" (Behar, 1996, p. 14).

Consider for illustration the discussion of Patrice's practical and research purposes in Chapter 2. For Patrice (hypothetically speaking) to foreground her critical stance and stipulate as the purpose of her study the "empowerment of Early Head Start families" or the "reconfiguration of power relationships between home visitors and their families" would create, as Rossman and Rallis (1998) suggest, "some tricky cognitive dissonance" (p. 79). As these authors argue, researchers cannot simply mandate or stipulate things like empowerment, however strongly they feel about it. They can, however, convey how their inquiry may (and perhaps should) *create the capacity* for understanding and valuing the ways in which participants might become empowered or how relationships might be changed.

Chapter 9 will include consideration of how your intellectual and moral perspectives find expression as you shift from the largely discovery-focused process of conceptualization to the largely presentation-focused documentation of this process in the form of a proposal.

SUMMARY

Researchers cannot meaningfully engage a study without some idea of how, and from what perspective, they are focusing on the topic of their inquiry. In this chapter we addressed the process of developing an intellectual identity for yourself as a researcher and, in particular, positioning yourself relative to a paradigm or worldview. This positioning entails, first, defining a *stance* for yourself by committing to a basic set of beliefs; second, considering the lens through which you will filter these beliefs; and third, articulating how these first two processes might lead you to identify with a particular frame of reference (paradigm or worldview). The frame of reference from which you view your inquiry represents a conscious choice that informs and extends your research aims, including how, and by whom, your data are interpreted and put to use. This choice is also shaped by the degree to which you want or need to be involved during fieldwork in social, ethical, and emotional terms, a topic we will revisit in Chapter 8.

The perspective you bring to your research is not a banner you wave overhead or a badge you wear conspicuously on your sleeve. Its influence is pervasive but subtle, even as you shift from the exploratory and position-building emphases of conceptualization to the justifying and audience-directed emphases of a research proposal (see Chapter 9).

CHAPTER 4

CONSTRUCTING A CONCEPTUAL CONTEXT

How do my ideas about what's important fit with other people's ideas about what's important? What am I doing about theory? Have I built a sound argument for proceeding with my inquiry?

Time now to address an assumption that has underlain your sense of problem and purpose since your initial efforts to shape your inquiry. That assumption is one of coherence. *Coherence,* following Agar (1996), does not refer to a rigid framework of ideas, nor does it mean the absence of speculation or uncertainty. What it does mean is this: You are assuming a point of view, a way of thinking and seeing, a context for your inquiry in terms of which your problem, and your reasons and strategies for pursuing it, make sense.

Your task as you consider this aspect of conceptualizing and shaping your inquiry is to give explicit form and substance to that context. This means that you need to establish the *conceptual integrity* of your inquiry, to make a case for how and why your ideas matter relative to a significant, accumulating body of knowledge.

SEEKING THEORETICAL LEGITIMACY

Patrice's confidence that she had identified a research problem of personal and scholarly importance was matched by her desire that others regard her study as theoretically legitimate, not to judge it as "conceptually thin." Establishing herself theoretically, part of the task in developing a conceptual context, highlighted a twofold challenge:

> . . . on the one hand to come up with an original problem and a theoretically adequate approach to it, on the other hand to be able to demonstrate how a unique case is embedded in some larger concern related to a significant body of theory. (Wolcott, 1995, p. 183)

Viewed in this way, Patrice's conceptual context served as a point of entry for her to address questions of:

- **significance** ("How is my inquiry, and the manner in which I am approaching it, important?")

- **situatedness**   ("How does my inquiry fit within a broader array of significant ideas?")
- **transferability**   ("How might my inquiry contribute to an understanding of similar issues in other settings?")

The task of constructing a conceptual context was thus posed: to generate a broader context for understanding her particular inquiry by linking it conceptually to some accumulating body of knowledge.

Thinking Theoretically

Among the more daunting aspects of this task is dealing with the issue of theory. We can identify theory along a continuum that extends from formal explanatory axiom (Bowlby's Infant Attachment Theory), to tentative hunch ("Something about that interaction between mother and infant doesn't seem right"), to any general set of ideas that guide action ("It's more appropriate to ask the mother about it first").

The common assumption is that we need theory, at some level, to lend a certain legitimacy and purpose to what we do as researchers. While it is affirming to be able to assert one's status as a researcher by claiming, "My theory is. . . ," theory can contribute to your work in several practical ways:

- **Connectedness:**   Theory offers a way to join your work to some larger issue or body of knowledge, in part by inviting you to consider classes of events rather than only single instances.
- **Critique:**   Theory offers a critical (in its broadest sense) perspective by directing attention to prior work "in which certain aspects of a problem may have been singled out because they have been inadequately attended to or have raised new doubts or concerns" (Wolcott, 1995, p. 189).
- **Purposefulness:**   Theory helps you avoid opportunistic study of "everything" by linking broader principles and perspectives with your decisions to attend to some things but not others in the course of your inquiry (Sanjek, 1991).

Conversely, what you need to avoid is the tight embrace of theory as a singular preoccupation in your work. Imposing a well-established theory on your developing inquiry may set you up with a neat and satisfying framework for your study, but may prematurely shut down avenues of meaningful questioning or prevent you from seeing events and relationships that don't fit the theory. As one experienced researcher suggested, "Theory does not determine the fieldwork experience, but it may provide the dictionary with which it is read" (Van Maanen, 1988, pp. 97–98).

Theory as a Way of Asking

These general considerations beg the question of precisely when and how theory should play a role in your work. In addressing this question, you might begin by regarding your conceptual context itself as a theory of sorts, or in Maxwell's (1996) words, "a formulation of what you think is going on with the phenomena you are studying" (p. 25). However anxiety-producing this notion of conceptual context as theory might be to you as a novice researcher, consider its practical expression in this definition proposed by Wolcott (1995): "Theory is a way of asking that is accompanied by a reasonable answer" (p. 186). He explains:

> If the research problem you intend to pursue is accompanied by a reasonable answer, you can proceed more-or-less theoretically, more if your "answer" is linked to some larger body of thought and prior work, less if the answer is your own modest hunch or hypothesis. Recognize, however, that you can proceed with fieldwork without a reasonable answer to the question(s) you are asking, as long as you have a reasonable sense of how to proceed, how to focus your attention. (p. 187)

As described in the context of Patrice's entry-level theorizing (Chapter 2), something as casual as an intuitive sense that "something is not right" in a social situation might be sufficient to set off purposeful inquiry. When and how theory becomes *more* or *less* a matter of explicit concern within your inquiry can be answered, in part, by drawing upon the useful distinction between *significant theories* and *theories of significance* (Sanjek, 1991).

Significant Theories and Theories of Significance

Thinking theoretically may or may not entail making *a* theory explicit and formal, as, for example, when you enlist a set of principles that is well established in the literature and perhaps even associated with an individual's name (e.g., Kohlberg's Theory of Moral Development). Theories at this "big T" level—Sanjek's (1991) *significant theories*—relate what you intend to do in the field to the larger constellation of ideas and issues brought into focus by your inquiry. Theory in this sense provides something of a legitimizing and narrowing influence upon the wide-ranging trajectories of hunches, tentative musings, and other forms of entry-level theorizing in which you have engaged. As illustrated in a later section of this chapter, Patrice filtered her definition of problem and purpose, with all the accompanying entry-level hunches and tentative musings, through the concept-rich categories of infant mental health, early intervention, and culture theory.

In addition to significant theories, field-oriented researchers develop *terrain-specific theories of significance* (Sanjek, 1991) to help them accomplish what they want to accomplish relative to the people, processes, and places that comprise their fieldwork. *Terrain-specific* refers to the idea that you are making judgments of significance on a local or immediate level—that is, you are generating modest "little t" theories that enable you to take a particular slice of experience and make sense of it by putting it into context. *Context* here refers both to how your "little t" theory relates to other events in the immediate setting and to how it relates to any larger significant theories you have enlisted. Recall, for example, Patrice's entry-level theorizing about the infant in the restaurant and how that interaction played off established understandings of healthy and age-appropriate behavior.

Whether or not you are all that explicit about the theoretical dimensions of your inquiry, a basic rule of thumb is that, as a researcher, you must know what you are up to and be able to explain to others what this is. To this end, you should embrace theory to the extent that it is useful in serving your purposes, not the other way around and not simply for show. Thinking in terms of a conceptual context for your inquiry allows you to be relatively modest when making claims about the ideas you are weaving into your work, while also inviting (but not demanding) consideration of how these ideas may fit into some broader theoretical scheme. As a matter of practice, you might pose the question:

> What do I need by way of theory—or more modestly, by way of concepts—to help me to make sense of, and develop a sound argument for, what I am doing, how I am going about it, and what I am choosing to attend to in my fieldwork?

FORMULATING AN ARGUMENT

At a fundamental level—that is, at a modest level relative to claims about theory—your aim in constructing a conceptual context is to develop a working argument that says,

- "Here's how I am positioning my problem within an established arena of ideas," and
- "Here's why that matters."

Constructing this argument is a generative process that calls for something more than a neatly packaged description of ideas that have influenced your thinking. You need to make a contestable case for how your inquiry matters relative to a larger landscape of ideas. Constructing an argument is also a selective process, in which the central issue is how effectively you make use of existing research, concepts, and theories, including your own experiential knowledge, to launch the research question(s) that will set you on a particular trajectory of inquiry.

The biggest risk lies in equating this formative task with the customary summative effort associated with a traditional review of the literature. With an eye toward the former, consider how you might respond to the following issues and questions in the course of developing your argument:

- **Authority:** Am I treating the literature as "a useful but fallible source of *ideas* about what's going on" or as "an *authority* to be deferred to" (Maxwell, 1996, p. 27)?
- **Focus:** Am I engaging directly and meaningfully with my problem by drawing on the relevant work of others on a "when-and-as-needed" basis (Wolcott, 2001, p. 74), or am I simply plowing through, and then parading, everything I can find on this topic?
- **Ownership:** Are the concepts and theories in the literature serving my purposes or the other way around?
- **Purposefulness:** Is my argument leading toward a meaningful research question or toward some neat and tidy, self-fulfilling explanation and solution?
- **Comprehensiveness:** Is my argument helping me to see alternative ways of framing the issues?

- **Credibility:**   How is my argument helping to establish my credibility as a researcher who should be considering these ideas and pursuing this inquiry?

The crucial point, following Maxwell (1996) in particular, is that a conceptual context is something you construct, not something that is waiting passively out there in the literature, intact and ready-made as a framework for your particular inquiry. Developing your conceptual context does not mean trying to cover everything that has been written about a topic; nor does it mean relying entirely on an existing theory as a conceptual container in which you try to fit all your insights and arguments. Rather, the task is one of uncovering what is relevant and what is problematic among the ideas circling around your problem, making new connections, and then formulating an argument that positions you to address that problem in a particular way. Let's consider how conceptual context as theory building might look in practice.

DIRECTING THE FLOW OF IDEAS

Identifying Currents of Thought

In developing her conceptual context, Patrice suggested a simple but elegant notion, "currents of thought," to describe the categories of knowledge that informed her argument. *Current* is an apt term that encompasses both the distinct flow of a category of ideas and the capacity for those ideas to join (flow into) related categories. In Patrice's case, the three currents of infant mental health, early intervention, and culture theory each presented a means for her to uncover and connect with issues relevant to the problem she had defined.

Her search of the literature and her prior research in these three areas extended no further than she needed to establish meaningful conceptual linkages between a particular category of knowledge and the problem she was proposing to study. Conceptual linkages can refer to:

- insights from prior research or theory that support or extend an idea with which you are working.
- perceived problems with prior research or theory.
- contradictions, paradoxes, or gaps in existing perspectives.
- ways in which one's concerns might extend current thinking about what's going on with an issue or topic.

Use of the term *meaningful* refers directly to the issues of authority, focus, ownership, and purposes, as described earlier in this section. It also refers to one's ability to engage, rather than simply fall in line with, ideas in the literature. Your aim at this juncture is to work through these ideas and channel them into focused lines of questioning.

Channeling Your Ideas into Lines of Inquiry

This speculative aspect of the process is the means through which your currents of thought start to flow into each other. You've done some of the uncovering work and are taking a more deliberate step toward making new connections and formulating an argument relative to your research problem.

To illustrate, some of the key issues (meaningful conceptual linkages) that emerged for Patrice as she moved along the currents of her conceptual work included the following:

- The literature on infant development does not reflect a notion of infant well-being that takes into account the social and economic diversity of U.S. society (*"infant mental health" current*).
- Professionals in the fields of infant development and early intervention apply concepts of emotional health and development created outside the social and economic contexts of the families to which they are often applied, particularly in the determination of eligibility for human service programs like Early Head Start (*"early intervention" current*).
- Current diversity paradigms place an emphasis on ethnicity at the expense of social and economic considerations. Notions of what it means to work in families' "natural environments" tend not to encompass ways of being that are related to the values and beliefs of those who are different from the mainstream (*"culture theory" current*).

Taken together, these three examples encapsulate what were, at various points in time, anywhere from 15 to 30-some pages in which Patrice played her thought-about positions (see Chapter 2) off her selective analyses and critiques of the literature. *Play* is the operative term here, in the sense of encouraging creative, exploratory thinking—what Maxwell (1996) calls "thought experiments"—with the aim of generating speculative "if . . . then . . . " types of questions or propositions focused on the implications of approaching one's problem in a certain way. This is conceptual context *as* theory building, a way of asking accompanied by a reasonable and arguable answer.

As you consider the following examples generated by Patrice in her conceptual work, keep in mind that these are not her research questions. Rather, these are lines of speculation and inquiry that direct attention to the pivotal concerns of her inquiry. Think of them as the conceptual underpinnings of her (still to be formulated) research question(s).

- "If parents and social groups have differing goals for their children based on the socially determined competencies necessary for survival in a group, then what are the values and behaviors of families who live in chronic poverty that adults reward and pass on to their children?"
- "If infants' and toddlers' day-to-day environmental experiences most strongly predict later well-being and competence, then maybe 'we' (mainstream Americans) don't like the implications for expanding our conceptualization of who we are because it may weaken our perceived competence as a whole."
- "If cultural models provide individuals with understandings of what is 'right' and 'natural,' then what does that imply about the perceived value of those who cannot achieve what is right or natural?"

- "If the children who are raised in socially and economically different contexts are perceived as less competent than those in the American mainstream, then they are likely never to be included in the aggregate; they will continue to be 'outsiders' and may not succeed in school."
- "If, however, we can understand children's experiences in terms of their contexts and see their competencies as revealed in these experiences, then I wonder if school success might follow."

The delineation of pivotal concerns in the form of "if. . . then" types of questions or propositions provides an effective way of wrapping up one's conceptual context. Considered in relationship with each other, these concerns convey how you have established yourself theoretically and then set you up for considering the nature and substance of the research question(s) that will guide your inquiry. Chapter 9 will address how these pivotal concerns reemerge to inform and find specific expression within the Conceptual Context/Theoretical Orientation section and the Research Questions section of your research proposal document.

Opening the Way for More

While the assumption of coherence, as addressed at the start of this chapter, may imply a sense of completeness, what it really calls for is a sense of connectedness between and among ideas. In building the connections that underlie your philosophical and conceptual contexts, you are making the claim that, however modest in scope your particular inquiry may be, it does relate in meaningful ways to broader perspectives and issues. This is an essential point in your claim to a qualitative stance: Through your context building, you are opening the way to present your problem and your research question as something that is *more,* rather than *less,* complex (Peshkin, 1988; Wolcott, 1999).

SUMMARY

Making a case for how and why your idea matters relative to a significant body of knowledge is the essence of constructing a conceptual context. This is a generative and selective process in which you uncover what is relevant and what is problematic among the ideas circling around your problem, and then formulate an argument that positions you to address that problem in a particular way. Your conceptual context thus serves as a means to address questions pertaining to your inquiry's significance, situatedness, and transferability. Determining when and how theory plays a role in your

thinking is a key aspect of establishing the conceptual integrity of your work.

Each aspect of identity and context building, philosophical (Chapter 3) and conceptual, informs and enriches the other, contributing to the overall sense of connectedness among the ideas that shape your inquiry. Both are crucial to understanding decisions you will make about how to formulate your research question(s) (Chapter 5), distinguish and decide among approaches to fieldwork (Chapter 6), consider strategies in anticipation of fieldwork (Chapter 7), and establish the integrity of your inquiry (Chapter 8).

FORMING RESEARCH QUESTIONS

How do I take the ideas that I have filtered through my problem, purpose, perspective, and conceptual context and transform them into a meaningful research question? And once I form a question, how do I determine whether it is the right question to be pursuing?

Moving your inquiry toward a point of clear definition in the form of a research question is the focus of this chapter. As you have likely determined from the preceding chapters, getting at a research question is not like driving down a clearly marked road to a scenic destination according to a travel club's map. Rather it is something closer in kind to the preliminary give-and-take discussion you have with yourself and others about whether, where, why, and how you might want to go somewhere—interactive, spiraling, but not without points of reference.

In order to help you identify your points of reference and move toward an appropriate and workable research question, I have organized this chapter around the following issues and orienting concerns:

- **Moving Toward Your Question**

    Orienting Concern #1: Tacking Between Breadth and Precision

    Key Question: How do you negotiate the many different questions and issues swirling around your topic to "get at" a worthwhile research question?

    Orienting Concern #2: Attending to What Matters

    Key Question: Does it matter whether your inquiry is driven by a single, central research question or by several questions?

- **Justifying Your Question**

    Orienting Concern #3: Assessing Goodness of Fit

    Key Question: How do you determine whether your research question is a "good fit" for what you want to understand?

    Orienting Concern #4: Orienting and Rationalizing Your Approach

    Key Question: How do you determine whether your research question is the right question to be asking as a qualitative researcher?

• Going Somewhere with Your Question

Orienting Concern #5: Defining the Evolution of Your Inquiry

Key Question: What does it mean for the question that you bring to the research setting to "evolve" during the course of your inquiry?

MOVING TOWARD YOUR RESEARCH QUESTION

Orienting Concern #1: Tacking Between Breadth and Precision

Key Question: How do you negotiate the many different questions and issues swirling around your topic to "get at" a worthwhile research question?

In the introduction to Part One I described the research question as one of a number of mutually responsive components—engaging with a sense of problem, clarifying purposes, establishing an intellectual orientation and moral stance, developing a conceptual context—in a dynamic process of conceptualizing and generating your study. Following Maxwell (1996) and my own experience, I argued that research questions are in most cases the result of an interactive design process rather than being the starting point for that process. This discussion helped to establish how your research questions give specific shape to your stated purposes and make explicit that which you want to learn.

With this basic understanding in mind, consider the situation of Deb, a student at the point of defining the question that would guide her study. Deb's introduction to graduate work in qualitative research coincided with her responsibilities as Director of the Academic Support Center at a private, two-year, post-secondary institution. The support center was a place where students could receive additional academic assistance in the form of peer tutoring and faculty support. Deb's proposed research was rooted in her perception that the center's programs failed to provide adequate support for some students; for others, the center provided too much support, effectively taking away students' ownership of their own work. She was concerned that the "equal educational opportunity" promised for these students by the college was, as she stated, "merely the illusion of an opportunity."

Where and how does she proceed to identify her central research question? Does she start at the conceptual or theoretical level and try a "big picture" approach to her problem (e.g., sorting through conflicting perspectives on "equal educational opportunity," as explored in her conceptual context)? Or, does she focus first on small, discrete pieces—detailed slices of life—that could give more definite shape to her question but might just as easily turn out to be irrelevant (e.g., asking why some students are expressing frustration about their classroom experience or why some faculty are expressing frustration about their students' performance)?

Both of these seemingly contrary ways of perceiving and proceeding through inquiry inform the qualitative perspective. For researchers like Deb, the dual ability to "peer broadly" while attending to the nitty-gritty of the particular (Peacock, 1986) provides a way of homing in on a well-formulated research question. In practical terms, this means tacking continuously between questions that address "What's the big picture here?" and those that address "What, in particular, is going on here?" until these complementary lines of inquiry converge as a single image around which the researcher can wrap his or her research question. This is the familiar rhythm of qualitative inquiry, a sort of "intellectual perpetual motion" (Geertz, 1984, p. 134) between *breadth of vision* and *precision of focus.*

Example 5.1 offers a glimpse into how this dialectical tacking between breadth and precision played out in Deb's case. I have developed this example from working

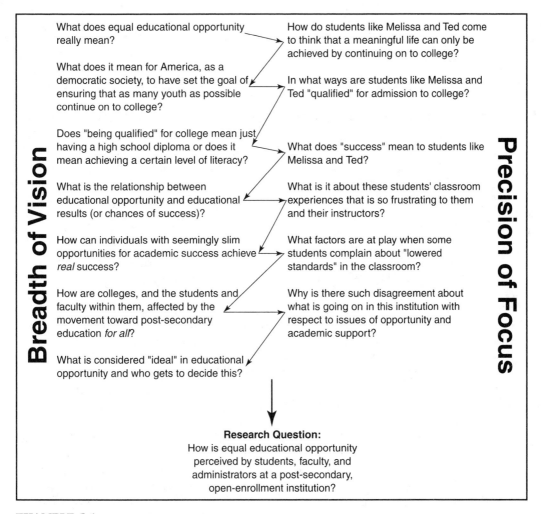

EXAMPLE 5.1
Moving Toward a Research Question: A study of equal educational opportunity in higher education

questions and "If . . . then . . . " formulations that Deb addressed as she worked through the conceptual context for her inquiry (see Chapter 4). These questions and others like them served as her key reference points as she sought to give specificity and direction to her research purpose in the form of a central research question.

The stated purpose of Deb's study at this point in the process was "to better understand the notion of *real* educational opportunity in higher education." If we examine the questions emphasizing breadth of vision in Example 5.1, we see Deb trying to make conceptual or theoretical connections between educational opportunity and assumptions people have made about its value, its ties with individual achievement, the nature of success, and so on. If we examine the same issue emphasizing precision of focus, we see "reality check" types of questions that highlight the particularity of lived or observed experiences. Keep in mind that this is not a linear process, but rather a dialectical one in which questions from both sides play off and inform each other.

Orienting Concern #2: Attending to What Matters

Key Question: Does it matter whether your inquiry is driven by a single, central research question or by several questions?

For qualitatively oriented research, in which one is never quite sure where to set the boundaries of relevant context, there can be a different twist to the challenge described in the previous section. In many cases, especially early on, your "tacking" may lead you to the decision that your inquiry is best served not by one but by several research questions.

While researchers tend to agree that trying to work from more than a few major research questions is looking for trouble—what Miles and Huberman (1994) discuss as "research question proliferation"—there is no solid consensus on whether it is best to proceed from one or several research questions. Nor is there agreement, if the decision is made to use a number of questions, on whether each question holds the same status or function in one's inquiry (Are some actually subquestions? Do they build on each other in a linear or logical fashion? If not, how *do* they complement each other?).

Creswell (1998), for example, recommends that a researcher "reduce his or her entire study to a single, overarching question and several subquestions" (p. 99). Stake (1995), specifically addressing case study research, offers a model that distinguishes between *issue* questions and *topical* questions. The former provide the conceptual structure for organizing one's inquiry by addressing major problematic concerns. The latter address anticipated needs for information as, for example, questions that relate to a description of the context. Miles and Huberman (1994) suggest drafting and iterating a set of six or seven general research questions and, over time, honing a smaller number of major questions, each with specific subquestions. They leave open the possibility of drawing out a "key question" from this process.

Consider the experience of another student, Linda, who began by drafting the following set of five (or more, depending on how you distinguish them) general research questions. The purpose of the study, in her words, was "to describe the experiences of Asian American students as they pertain to racial and ethnic identity development in a predominantly white, small college setting." She settled herself into her inquiry with the intent of generating an explanation of identity formation, with a dual focus on individual self-identification and the sociologic processes involved in group membership. The following questions, including the manner in which they are grouped, emerged from an early draft of her research design:

1. How do Asian American students construe their identities in a rural, elite college environment? How do they self-identify and what meaning do they attach to these identities?

2. What have been the experiences of Asian Americans in this community (primarily students but also including faculty and administrators)? What roles have race and ethnicity played in the lives of these individuals?

3. What types of communities do the students come from? What factors within their home communities played important roles in the development of racial and ethnic identity prior to college?

4. In which communities do the students participate in college? What factors within the students' college-based communities play an important role in the development of racial and ethnic identity during college?

5. What is the role of the institution, and how does it affect the experiences of Asian American students?

At first glance, Linda's listing of what are actually nine distinct questions might seem to put her at risk of losing the forest for the trees, overly fragmenting the way she approaches data collection. But laying out her questions in this preliminary manner proved to be an eminently productive strategy for her as she sought to articulate more precisely the nature and focus of her inquiry. In particular, it placed in stark relief the crucial distinction noted by Maxwell (1996), Stake (1995), and others between questions that formulate what you want to understand and questions you ask in order to gain that understanding.

In Linda's case, all of the questions listed under numbers 2 to 5 (and to some degree the second question in number 1) are closer in kind to the topical questions that cover anticipated needs for information and, in practical terms, feed directly into the specific questions she would ask as an interviewer and observer in the field. Reconsidered as a "topical outline" (Stake, 1995), for example, these questions (or subquestions, if you prefer) served to foreshadow and actually set into motion procedures of data collection and analysis (Creswell, 1998). Sorting through her questions in this fashion, Linda eventually identified her key research question as it rose to the surface—a version of the first question in number 1. This question could not be directly operationalized or translated into a question she might ask to guide an interview or observation, but it did serve the broader purpose of directing attention to the issue she really wanted to understand.

The winnowing aspect of this process serves well to remind us that the critical and ongoing task for qualitative inquirers is not, as might be expected, to try to account for everything (as suits our inclination to set few limits on what we can uncover through our investigations). Rather, as Wolcott (1988) pointedly reminds us, it

Central Question #1
What is the meaning of infant well-being from the perspective of families who participate in Early Head Start services?

Central Question #2
What is the experience of families who participate in Early Head Start?

Topical Questions
How do parents understand infant development—do they see themselves as having the ability to influence development, or do they attribute development to factors outside their locus of control?

How do parents understand the context of infant development—the relationship between themselves and their infants, and the influence of environmental factors on the development of their infants?

Do parents have goals and priorities for their infants? If they do, are they able to identify and articulate them? Which goals do they hold most dear?

What values and beliefs do parents pass on to their children? To what extent are these imbued in the experiences that infants have with their families?

Topical Questions
Are there implicit goals that home visitors bring to the relationship? If so, what are they? How do these goals influence the relationship, if they do?

What is the process of relationship building that unfolds between home visitors and their partner families? What helps or hinders this process of relationship building? How do families perceive the "help giving" that is intended by their home visitor?

What meaning do families ascribe to having a home visitor? What do the families perceive to be the implications of participating in the home visiting component of Early Head Start?

EXAMPLE 5.2
Central Research Questions and Their Topical Subquestions: A study of infant well-being from the perspective of families impacted by poverty

is to "try to get *rid* of almost everything, of honing the topic and sharpening the focus, so that increasingly there is *less* to be concerned with, and thus what is of concern can be observed with greater attention" (p. 27).

Example 5.2 illustrates the working relationship between central research questions and their topical subquestions. Here again I draw from Patrice's study of infant well-being from the perspectives of families participating in Early Head Start. Note how her topical questions establish a sequence of inquiry that builds incrementally and logically toward her central concerns, as expressed in her two research questions. Her topical questions also served the aim of setting in motion what she might actually do and say in the field setting.

JUSTIFYING YOUR RESEARCH QUESTION

Orienting Concern #3: Assessing Goodness of Fit

Key Question: How do you determine whether your research question is a "good fit" for what you want to understand?

A useful step in confirming the "rightness" of your research question is to develop a set of responses to questions about the logic and reasoning that helped to shape it. The following questions can help you frame an argument that addresses how your research question works for you and why it makes sense.

- Is my research question working to address my problem?
- How am I deciding whether my question is too focused or too broad?
- How have I checked for assumptions that may be embedded in my question?
- On what basis can I claim that my research question is answerable?

Figure 5.1
Thinking Through Your Research Question

Assessing the goodness of fit between your research question and what you want to understand by doing the study is a necessary step in establishing a coherent inquiry. It also gets at the heart of what you can and should expect a qualitative research question to do for you. The issue here is what we might call the *responsiveness* of your research question: how well it "answers" your problem, purpose, focus, and assumptions and what implicit claim it makes of being an answerable question in the first place.

In a manner that reflects the more comprehensive process of constructing a conceptual context for a study (see Chapter 4), you might find it useful to delineate what you think is going on with your research question. Specifically, consider in systematic fashion how you might respond to a set of queries that address how your research question works for you and why it makes sense. The questions and issues summarized in Figure 5.1 can help you think through your research question and assess its goodness of fit.

Is my research question working to address my problem?
The underlying issue: Convincing readers that your study is worthwhile plays off your ability to situate your research as addressing a particular, important problem (Marshall & Rossman, 1999). Defining the problem, of course, is a first step in shaping your study's significance, but it is in demonstrating a problem that your study's significance is affirmed. Your research question provides the crucial link between these two aims.

For illustration, consider again the trajectory of questions posed by Deb in her study of educational opportunity (Example 5.1). We can see embedded in her line of inquiry the growing sense that things are not quite right as they are or, at the least, are not as good as they might be. Also underlying her questions is an increasing awareness of circumstances under which educational opportunity might be considered problematic. Eventually, more in character with a raised eyebrow than a pointing finger, her central research question emerges, inviting consideration of the situation as something other than the way things appear to be or are expected to be.

Purposeful, but avoiding prediction, Deb's central research question helps to address her problem by appropriately anticipating the possibility that a problem exists, in this case, around how different people in the setting understand educational opportunity. In basic terms, then, we can view the "work" of the research question as *creating the capacity for problem finding* in the setting.

How am I deciding whether my question is too focused or too broad?

The underlying issue: What is at stake here is the role of your research question in indicating what, and how much, you are likely to attend to in your study. Practicality is a major consideration when determining one's scope of inquiry, of course, but even this can be a fuzzy standard in an approach so uniquely suited to uncovering the unexpected and exploring leads as they emerge. Herein lies a tension. Your research question should be flexible enough to permit exploration but focused enough to delimit the study (Marshall & Rossman, 1999).

Care must be taken when attempting to heed the general advice to keep your focus as broad as possible for as long as possible when entering into a qualitative field study. While such openness is the hallmark of qualitative methods, it does not obligate you to formulate a research question that remains at the preliminary "What's going on here?" level.

Conversely, caution should be also used when considering the advice (commonly directed at the novice) to "think small." Thinking small, Bogdan and Biklen (1998) remind us, means thinking about practical limitations as you formulate your question; it does *not* mean making your research question overly specific. Among other considerations, they argue, a question that is too specific may cause difficulty for the qualitative researcher because the issues posed may not arise in the time available for studying them. An example of such a question would be, "How do teachers incorporate models of peer coaching into their first year of teaching?" Questions that are too focused may also lead you to not pay attention early on to a wide enough range of data, thereby leading you to overlook important but unanticipated findings (Maxwell, 1996).

Marshall and Rossman (1999) address the issue of focus by presenting a useful categorization of types of initial research questions. While not exhaustive or accounting for the overlapping of categories, their examples do provide one way of thinking about how one's initial research question can serve to bound a study without unduly constraining it.

- **Theoretical questions**   can be researched in a number of different sites or with different samples. Examples include:

  - How does play affect reading readiness?
  - How does the mentoring process function in the socialization of professionals?

- Questions focused on **particular populations** can also be studied in various places but direct attention to a particular person, group, or class of individuals. Examples include:

  - What happens to women who enter elite MBA programs?
  - How do first-year teachers perceive their relations with their more experienced colleagues?

- **Site-specific**   questions seek to highlight the uniqueness of a particular program or organization. Examples include:

  - How do grassroots environmentalist groups in coastal New Hampshire influence practices among local commercial fisherman?
  - How do home-school relations of an elite private school differ from those in the neighboring public school?

A basic consideration when determining whether your question is too diffuse or too focused is to assess its effectiveness in serving as a guide for decisions you need to make as you prepare to enter the field and actually conduct your study. An appropriately focused question should foreshadow and actually set into motion procedures of informant selection, data collection, and analysis (Creswell, 1998).

How have I checked for assumptions that may be embedded in my question?
The underlying issue: Assumptions are inevitably and insistently present throughout the process of inquiry. They represent an invariable component of research that is not inherently good or bad but that does impact how you pose questions and conduct fieldwork. Left unexamined, assumptions may lead you to focus on what you *think* is going on in a setting and prevent you from seeing what is actually happening. Giving your assumptions the meaningful attention they deserve can make you aware of how they may be shaping your inquiry and its outcomes (Glesne, 1999; Peshkin, 1988).

Tim, a graduate student in mathematics education, undertook a case study of how a mathematician who had just completed a Ph.D. was socialized into his first university faculty position. His research focused on the question of how being a mathematician and "doing mathematics" influenced the ways in which the newcomer learned about and adapted to the values and practices of his new departmental work setting.

In early drafts of his write-up, Tim revisited a key assumption that influenced the way he presented his problem and posed his research questions. He wrote:

> *Questions posed in preparation for this study were all predicated on the belief that department members would be "doing mathematics." If I asked, "How do these people measure success?" I was really asking, "How do these people, who have a professional life built around doing mathematics, measure success?"*

As Tim conceptualized it, "doing mathematics" meant engaging in mathematical activity for rewards that were intrinsically mathematics related: either enjoyment of the process itself or recognition as a mathematician. The assumption that underlay his central research question was that this type of engagement was necessarily a part of any new faculty member's socialization into a mathematics department. It was not until he was several months into his fieldwork that Tim realized the assumed significance of doing mathematics was both irrelevant and potentially misleading for describing what was actually going on in the setting (namely, a lot of talk about how to teach and deal with students).

Clyde Kluckhohn is reputed to have once stated, "If a fish were an anthropologist, the last thing it would discover would be water." Assumptions often work this way—that is, their impact can be felt as a consequence of the familiar being all too familiar. Tim was a mathematician "fish" in his own element. His research question, built around the notion of doing mathematics, served to reinforce what he thought must or should be going on in a community of mathematicians. His assumption kept him focused on an aspect of mathematicians' lives that was true in some cases (including, no doubt, his own experience) but was not valid for the case on which he was focused for his study. Consequently, he spent a great deal of time looking for something that wasn't there and, as he describes, had to revisit the emphasis in his original research question:

> For a good deal of the time on site I struggled with the question of how to pursue my original research questions in a setting in which, based on my definition, mathematics was not being done. To get at how mathematics is important in shaping the social interactions of department members, and how it influenced [my key informant's] enculturation process, required a different focus. Rather than looking at what mathematics people are doing, it became necessary to consider people's mathematical biographies, attitudes toward mathematics, and a variety of issues related to teaching mathematics.

For Tim, giving his assumptions the meaningful attention they deserved meant adopting a particular stance toward his inquiry—*making the familiar strange* (Eliot, 1950; Erickson, 1984; Salvio & Schram, 1995; Spindler & Spindler, 1982). The basic strategy entailed in making the familiar strange is to ask questions aimed at unearthing the taken-for-granted aspects of a situation, including assumptions that may be embedded in your research question itself (adapted from Erickson, 1984; Salvio & Schram, 1995):

- Why is this _____ (act, person, situation, concept, question) the way it is and not different?
- What am I leaving out (of my question) and what am I leaving in?
- What is the rationale for my selection of what's left out and what's left in?
- How might someone less familiar with this situation or problem interpret my research question?

On what basis can I claim that my research question is answerable?
The underlying issue: The issue here is straightforward: The data that could provide an answer for your question need to be obtainable through the means you have available. This, of course, raises practical concerns that pertain to available resources, time, access to a site or population, and the like—what Marshall and Rossman (1999) refer to as the "do-ability" of a study.

Underlying this level of practicality, the pivotal concern in addressing answerability is whether your question helps to establish a sense of *boundedness* for your study, a sense that your answers are not *out* there but rather are *some*where. To illustrate, consider the following question posed early on by Deb as she "tacked" toward a central research question for her study of educational opportunity (Example 5.1):

> What does it mean for America, as a democratic society, to have set the goal of ensuring that as many youth as possible continue on to college?

This question functioned well in the developmental role it played, namely, offering a view of the larger conceptual context and then angling Deb toward fresh grounding in a question tied to everyday realities. Had she tried to settle on this question to drive her study, however, it is difficult to envision how she would know where to start and how to proceed (beyond the general indicators of youth, college, and America). Now compare this earlier question with the one she settled upon to orient her study:

> How is equal educational opportunity perceived by students, faculty, and administrators at a post-secondary, open enrollment institution?

This comparison illustrates a fundamental consideration in assessing the claim of whether a research question is answerable: The question reserves enough flexibility to permit consideration of a range of answers (including unanticipated ones), but also sets, at least provisionally, the boundaries for fieldwork and analysis.

Orienting Concern #4: Orienting and Rationalizing Your Approach

Key Question: How do you determine whether your research question is the right question to be asking as a qualitative researcher?

The caution that Wolcott (1999) offers regarding the nature of an ethnographic question holds as well, and in only slightly varied form, for the art of posing questions in the broader context of qualitative inquiry. That is, you should not ask a qualitative question without some idea of what a qualitative answer looks like, some idea of the circumstances under which it does and does not make sense to pursue a qualitative approach beyond a commitment to fieldwork. The prerequisite condition is that you have formed a research question prior to the decision that your inquiry is best pursued by qualitative means. Remember: You choose a qualitative (or any type of) approach because of the nature of the research question, not vice versa. Following this basic premise, your research question has a dual role to play. It not only orients your movement down a qualitative path, but helps to rationalize it. That is, it embodies basic considerations that make a particular qualitative approach the more appealing and appropriate way to proceed with an inquiry.

The appeal of qualitative approaches is commonly attributed to the acknowledgment of multiple or partial truths, the need for contextual and holistic description and analysis, concern for the particular nature of occurrences rather than their general character and overall distribution, and the need to consider the meanings that happenings have for the people involved in them (as discussed in Chapter 1). In practical terms, these attributes suggest that qualitative fieldwork is well suited to answering the following types of questions (adapted from Erickson, 1986; Marshall & Rossman, 1999):

- What specific social actions and events are happening within this particular setting?
- What do actions, events, and ideas mean to the people engaged in and with them, and how do these understandings influence their behavior?
- How are events, actions, and meanings influenced by the particular context or unique circumstances in which they occur?
- How do happenings in the setting reflect patterns of behavior, meaning, or interaction? (Or, what plausible relationships are shaping what is happening?)
- How is what is happening in this setting as a whole (e.g., a classroom) related to happenings at other system levels within and beyond the setting (e.g., the school building, a child's family, the local community, federal immigration policies)?

Determining the appropriateness of a qualitative approach to your inquiry requires that you consider the nature of your research question and, in particular, the kind of understanding your study can generate. Maxwell (1992, 1996) offers a useful categorization of kinds of understanding in qualitative inquiry, emphasizing three that pertain most directly to the types of questions qualitative researchers ask:

- **descriptive**   questions that ask what is going on in terms of actual, observable (or potentially observable) events and behavior
- **interpretive**   questions that seek to explore the meaning of these things for the people involved
- **theoretical**   questions aimed at examining how these happenings can be explained

Qualitative research questions typically start with a *how* or a *what*. This should not be construed as part of some formulaic approach to the construction of research questions, but rather as a useful point of contrast to the *why, to what extent,* or *how much* questions for which qualitative studies are normally not appropriate. Regarding the latter choice of terms, qualitative studies rarely entail the sampling procedures or sample size that is required to generalize systematically to some wider population or context. So, too, are explicitly evaluative questions a risky and problematic way to orient an approach for which you are the primary research instrument. This does not mean, as Maxwell (1996) points out, "that you can never generalize or evaluate on the basis of

Table 5.1

The Fit Between Your Question and a Qualitative Approach

Well Suited to Qualitative Inquiry	Not Well Suited to Qualitative Inquiry
Questions aimed at:	*Questions aimed at:*
• documenting real events or cases bounded in time and circumstance	• testing relationships or establishing cause and effect
• understanding how participants in a setting make sense of and give meaning to their lives and experiences	• addressing the generality or wider prevalence of the phenomena being studied
• understanding contextual influences on actions and behaviors	• providing a comparison of groups or a relationship between variables, with the intent of establishing an association or cause and effect
• identifying unanticipated or taken-for-granted influences and phenomena	• predicting outcomes
• understanding processes by which events and actions take place	
• understanding the relationship between a particular scene and its wider social environments	

a qualitative study, only that such concerns are usually best *not* incorporated directly into your research questions" (p. 60). Table 5.1 distinguishes among various aims of research questions according to how well they are suited to a qualitative approach.

GOING SOMEWHERE WITH YOUR QUESTION

Orienting Concern #5: Defining the Evolution of Your Inquiry

Key Question: What does it mean for the question you bring to the research setting to "evolve" during the course of your inquiry?

"Given their complexity," writes Peshkin (1985), "field settings seldom contain a single point or story" (p. 214). Accordingly, it is a common expectation among qualitative researchers that their perspective will evolve in the course of sorting out what is central from what is peripheral to their inquiry. But does evolution of perspective necessarily mean evolution of the carefully formulated *question* you bring to the research setting? Once again, it depends.

Three fundamental points remain constant. First, as the inquirer, you own the first move. You create the question so that it communicates—in the way that good questions do—the heart of what you want to understand. Second, this first move is just that—an initial indicator that identifies what is primary in your research conception and that channels your energy in the direction of what you want to know most or need to know first. Third, an evolutionary orientation to one's inquiry is a good thing, *if,* by evolution, you mean to suggest change over time rather than progressive, linear improvement (Peshkin, 1985).

Patrice, whose experiences have figured prominently in the discussion up to this point, decided in the process of designing her study to orient her inquiry around two major research questions, as noted in Example 5.2. Her central questions reflected the twofold emphasis of her research, addressing, first, the concept of infant mental health and, second, the experience of participation in a program that provided services for families with infants:

1. What is the meaning of infant well-being from the perspective of families who participate in Early Head Start?
2. What is the experience of families who participate in Early Head Start?

The first question, Patrice reasoned, was intended to help her develop a "construct" of infant mental health derived from the meaning given to this notion by families impacted by poverty. It was important for her to understand the *perspective* of these families, she reasoned, because she was working from the assumption that these families do value the well-being of their babies but in ways she did not understand. Her second question was posed to provide information leading to an appraisal of Early Head Start for families who access the services. If families have different goals for their children based on culturally different ways of raising a baby, she reasoned, then understanding their experience in the program could illuminate barriers to their relationships with home visitors and increase the program's effectiveness. Although each question served in this early phase as a candidate for being the ultimate focusing issue of her inquiry, the potential also existed for a central question to evolve, as something of a hybrid, at the intersection of the two. Consider, for example, the following hypothetical outcomes:

- Patrice's first question leads to findings that suggest families impacted by poverty view infant well-being differently than middle class service providers in Early Head Start.
- Her second question leads to findings that suggest families who participate in Early Head Start experience persistent frustration when trying to convey their needs and questions about their infants' development to the service providers.
- After considering these findings, Patrice asks the question: "How are differing notions of infant well-being negotiated by families and service providers who participate in Early Head Start?"

The fitness and viability of this last question as a freshly honed focus for her research stem from when and how the question evolved. For Patrice, in this hypothetical scenario, the "differing notions" question was generated out of the dialectical process of linking ideas in her mind with what she observed and documented. This might be thought of as the *orienting phase* of field inquiry, a phase defined in large part by the deferral of judgment on what may be most significant to study in greater depth. In formulating her original two questions, Patrice had some notion of what was out there to be found, but the phrasing of these questions reflected a movement toward (not from) judgment; she did not merely set forth a prior, unsubstantiated hunch to be "tested" against data still to be gathered. In her emergent question, Patrice could ground—in solid data—her claim that differing views existed.

Does this mean that Patrice should substitute this last question for the first two as the central question in her research? Certainly not. The emergence of this question does not alter the fact that her research was driven initially by the first two questions; their original qualities and contributions are unimpaired by this reformulation. In particular, their significance in defining the evolution of her inquiry—and particularly, in reconstructing changes in her thinking about what was primary in her research conception—remains as vital as ever. The underlying point of this example is that your research questions serve a number of different functions, which vary in importance at different phases of the research.[1]

Another key issue here, and a defining one for qualitative inquiry, is how explicitly researchers distinguish between what they want (or need) to know and what they think is going on. Behind every question asked, there ought to be a working notion of *how* and *why* the answer to that question matters (Wolcott, 1995). This is different than embedding in your question a claim, however tentative, about what you think the answer might be. This distinction is crucial: the former encourages you to keep tabs on what you *don't* know; the latter may prevent you from seeing what's actually happening.

SUMMARY

In this chapter we addressed three major aspects of getting at and working with research questions. **Moving toward your question** is a dialectical process in which the researcher shifts creatively between questions that emphasize breadth of vision and precision of focus as a way to home in on a central research question. The winnowing aspect of this phase is built in part on the distinction between questions that formulate what you want to understand and questions that you actually ask in order to gain that understanding.

Justifying your question refers to how you assess the goodness of fit between your research question and what you want to understand by doing the study. Assessment of this fit includes consideration of the following: how your research question works to address your problem, how you decide whether your question is too focused or too broad, how you check for assumptions embedded in your question, and how you determine whether your question is answerable. The prerequisite condition to justifying your question is that you have

---

[1] I am grateful to Joseph Maxwell who, in his review of an earlier draft of this chapter, helped me to make this point more explicit.

formed your research question prior to the decision that your inquiry is best pursued by qualitative means.

Going somewhere with your question refers to how your perspective on a research question might evolve during the course of your study. A common expectation among qualitative researchers is that their perspective will evolve in the course of sorting out what is central from what is peripheral to their inquiry. A key issue in this sorting process is the distinction between what you want to know and what you think is going on or what you think the answer might be. Your research question should keep you focused on what is actually going on in a setting.

Research questions are in most cases the result of an interactive design process rather than the starting point for that process. They give specific shape to your stated purposes and make explicit what you want to learn.

CHAPTER 6

Making Decisions About Traditions

When and how should I distinguish and declare that I am working in a particular tradition of research? How do I decide which is the most appropriate tradition with which to align myself? Must I lay claim to a research tradition in its entirety, or can I draw upon selected aspects of it to guide my inquiry? How does the process of deciding how to identify my research approach help to clarify and strengthen my inquiry?

A central message of this chapter is conveyed by Kenneth Burke's oft-quoted statement, "A way of seeing is always a way of not seeing" (1935, p. 70). Your decision to commit yourself to or associate yourself with a particular research approach reflects the potential you believe to be gained from that perspective. An informed decision also takes into account the limitations or blind spots that commitment to a particular approach might entail.

The allure of affixing an impressive-sounding methodological label to the research you are doing is undeniable, drawn as we all are to the sense of comfort and validation that comes with being able to say "I'm doing an ethnography" or "I'm proceeding as a grounded theorist." Timing in this regard *does* matter, as does a discriminating eye. As noted in previous chapters, claiming a particular methodological label as a first step is inadvisable. Doing so suggests that your chosen research approach can serve as an all-purpose vehicle suitable for any problem, without apparent regard for what that problem or the accompanying research question might be.

The assumption underlying this chapter is that you are bringing to your methodological considerations the definition of problem, the clarity of purpose and perspective, and the focus of questions that enable you to establish the appropriateness of a particular research approach. The following sections proceed from this assumption and explore what it means to be an informed and discriminating decision maker when it comes time to claim a research tradition.

DEFINING RESEARCH TRADITIONS

My decision to attend to certain research traditions but not others in this chapter filters down to considerations of practicality, perception, and purpose. Qualitative researchers have never agreed among themselves about what to make of the differences and commonalities among their approaches, except to concur that there exists an almost baffling number of classifications or typologies from which to choose (see Chapter 1). My aim is not to try to resolve or account for these differing views, but to clarify how commitment to a particular research tradition predisposes you to a characteristic way of seeing and sets you up to achieve your purposes in certain ways.

Tradition vs. Method

It is important to maintain a clear distinction between research tradition and research method. When I speak of ethnography, grounded theory, and phenomenology as qualitative research *traditions,* I am defining them as rigorous, discipline-based, carefully specified ways to conceptualize, describe, and analyze human social behavior and processes (building on Wolcott, 1992, p. 37). Wolcott's (1999) useful distinction between a *way of seeing* (directing attention to perspective and intent) and a *way of looking* (directing attention to methods and procedures), although applied specifically to ethnography in his case, conveys the twofold nature of the definition I am using here.

To illustrate, phenomenology is not a method in and of itself, although it does incorporate specific methods. A study can be labeled phenomenological if it borrows techniques or methods associated with phenomenology. But a researcher should not claim to be *doing* phenomenology (or ethnography or grounded theory) solely on the basis of technique. Such claims rest more substantially on one's commitment to a research perspective that includes standards for what is worth knowing and how it is to be applied.

In accordance with this view I do not, for example, include action research or narrative research in my definition, although I remain a strong advocate of these approaches. Action research can and often does draw upon principles of ethnography, phenomenology, or grounded theory, among other approaches, in its conceptualization and construction, and historically it has used both quantitative and qualitative procedures (Creswell, 2002; Mills, 2000). In similar fashion, the genre of narrative research does not fall within the sole grasp of any specific disciplinary field but is claimed by a varying number of them (Rossman & Rallis, 1998, associate it with phenomenology, but not exclusively; also see Casey, 1995, 1996; Clandinin & Connelly, 2000). Narrative inquiry can be considered a category that encompasses a range of research practices, but such a wide embrace also contributes to substantial disagreement about its form (Clandinin & Connelly, 2000; Cortazzi, 1993; Creswell, 2002).

Similarly, the seemingly omnipresent case study does not implicate any particular approach. Although some scholars regard the case study as an identifiable method (e.g., Merriam, 1998; Stake, 1995; Yin, 1994), I follow Wolcott (2001) and others who regard it as an end product or format for reporting qualitative work. As such, it is not a distinct strategy or method; nor, by itself, is it a way of conceptualizing human social behavior and processes.

I also acknowledge that any distinctions I make place me on contested terrain, but my aim is to be illustrative rather than exhaustive around the issue of research traditions. Through a closer look at three influential and frequently used qualitative approaches—ethnography, grounded theory, and phenomenology—I hope to suggest how commitment to a particular methodological frame of reference influences and informs an inquiry in distinct ways.

The bulk of this chapter is devoted to helping you establish a basis for claiming some level of identification with a research approach. To this end, I have organized the discussion around key concerns of distinguishing among options and assessing goodness of fit, presenting each in a format of orienting questions.

DISTINGUISHING AMONG OPTIONS

What are some key distinguishing features of selected approaches to field-based qualitative research?

As suggested in the previous pages, distinctions among research traditions turn more on ways of seeing than ways of looking. Ways of looking—observing, asking, and examining what others have done—are notably similar across many qualitative research traditions. Ways of seeing—encompassing underlying intent, guiding concerns, focus, and perspective—are not so similar. To be an ethnographer, a phenomenologist, or a grounded theorist, you must develop a sense of what constitutes, respectively, an ethnographic, phenomenological, or grounded theory problem and question. Then you must come to terms with what concepts and assumptions guide an inquiry so that it results in that type of study. The considerations contained within these last two statements frame the following examination of research traditions.

Ethnography

The following summary draws upon the work of Agar (1996), Atkinson and Hammersley (1994), Brumann (1999), Emerson, Fretz, and Shaw (1995), Geertz (1984), Kuper (1999), LeCompte and Schensul (1999), Peacock (1986), and Wolcott (1999). For in-depth exploration of the following ideas I encourage you to consult these sources.

The Focus and Purpose of Ethnography

Unlike other forms of qualitative research, the defining characteristic of ethnography is that it is oriented toward the description and interpretation of *cultural* behaviors, as reflected in the following definition:

> The underlying purpose of ethnographic research . . . is to describe what the people in some particular place or status ordinarily do, and the meanings they ascribe to what they do, under ordinary or particular circumstances, presenting that description in a manner that draws attention to regularities that implicate cultural process. (Wolcott, 1999, p. 68)

The term *ethnography* represents both a process and a product. Ethnographic fieldwork, rooted in cultural anthropology and undertaken most commonly as participant observation, is the process by which a researcher comes to discern patterns and regularities—including patterned variations (Agar, 1996)—of behavior in human social activity. The process embraces multiple techniques, demands prolonged time in the field, and requires deep appreciation for the characteristic ethnographic tension of holding together corroborative, contrasting, and even incompatible perspectives as a necessary condition for documenting what is actually going on (Schram, 2000).

The ethnographic text, or product, is the means through which these cultural patterns, processes, and behaviors are interpreted and portrayed. Scholars generally agree that culture itself is not visible or tangible but is constructed by the act of ethnographic interpretation and writing (Kuper, 1999; Schwandt, 1997).

Basic Assumptions of the Ethnographer

- Human behavior and the ways in which people construct and make sense of their lives are highly variable and locally specific.
- Social behavior and interaction reflect varying patterns of what *should* occur (ideal behavior), what *does* occur (actual behavior), and what *might* occur (projective behavior).
- It is possible to discern these patterns of socially acquired and shared behavior through *experiencing* (observing and participating in people's lives and activities) and *inquiring* (asking people about their experiences and the meanings they ascribe to them).
- Before you can offer interpretations of people's actions and behaviors, you must uncover what they actually do and the reasons they give for doing it.
- The representation or interpretation that you construct of people's lives and behavior is neither "theirs" nor "yours." Instead, it is built upon the points of understanding and misunderstanding that occur between you and them.
- Ethnography cannot provide an exhaustive, absolute description of anything. Rather, ethnographic descriptions are necessarily partial, bound by what can be handled within a certain time, under specific circumstances, and from a particular perspective.

Orienting Concepts of Ethnography

Culture.   Culture is the knowledge that ethnographers construct "to show how acts in the context of one world can be understood as coherent from the point of view of another world" (Agar, 1996, p. 33). Viewed in this way, culture is an abstraction, an analytic framework that ethnographers apply to provide an underlying cohesiveness to their description of the clusters of common behaviors, concepts, and practices that arise when people interact regularly. Ethnographers can describe evidence of a certain *cultural pattern*—people sharing or withholding information as clues to their assumptions about power, for example—but culture itself remains an abstraction that they make based on such evidence. The fallacy lies in treating the abstraction, culture, as a concrete thing that can be observed firsthand or that can "do" this or that.

To describe culture as an abstraction is not to say that the attitudes, beliefs, and other acquired social behaviors that people manifest, which we categorize under the concept "culture," are not real; all of these human dispositions have reality and power in everyday experience. Nor does ethnography's overarching concern with cultural interpretation mean that an explicit cultural framework must be imposed on every study. But for a study to be ethnographic, it "must provide the kind of account of human social activity out of which cultural patterning can be discerned" (Wolcott, 1999, p. 68).

Holism or contextualization.   In describing what it means to "perceive holistically," anthropologist James Peacock (1986) tells the story of a Russian factory worker who habitually pushed his wheelbarrow through the factory gate at quitting time. Every evening the guards inspected the wheelbarrow and, after determining it was empty, let the worker pass. Months went by before it was discovered that the worker was stealing wheelbarrows. The guards' mistake, as Peacock explains, was to inspect the contents but not the carrier and his circumstances, to focus narrowly on the parts and not the whole, to fail to see holistically.

The concept of holism orients ethnographers toward an examination of things in their entirety rather than only in parts. Some ethnographers prefer the term *contextual* rather than holistic, although the two are not synonymous. The distinction is subtle but instructive. Holism seems to point to completeness or to the idea of something being greater than the sum of its parts. Contextualization suggests a more dynamic and dialectic process of making connections between parts and between parts and the whole (Agar, 1996; cf. Wolcott, 1999). Accordingly, instances of observed behavior make sense as part of a larger picture; in turn, that larger picture is continually brought into view through examination of its parts (Geertz, 1984).

This movement between parts and whole as a way of understanding both, which is central to ethnographic interpretation, can also refer to the trajectory of what is called the *hermeneutic circle.* Simply stated, and as originally applied to a text, the interpretation of each part depends on the interpretation of the whole, and vice versa. The notion of a *circle,* explains Schwandt (1997), highlights the idea that "every interpretation is itself based on another interpretation" (p. 64).

Holism is not, as Wolcott (1999) cautions, an invitation to "fill up" a study. Rather, a holistic and/or contextual perspective invites consideration of how parts and whole fit together so that ethnographers can "present human social behavior as *more,* rather than *less,* complex, to keep explanations from becoming simplistic or reductionist" (Wolcott, 1999, p. 79).

The Nature of Ethnographic Questions

Given the strong descriptive aspect of ethnography, ethnographic questions focus on what ethnographers are looking at and looking for in a particular context of human behavior and activity. By tradition and by design, ethnographic questions also position researchers to be especially attentive to the broad social context in which human behavior and activity occur.

Considered together, these seemingly opposing ways of posing questions—bringing into focus the encompassing milieu of an experience as well as the specific experience itself—inform ethnography's holistic perspective. Or, as framed in simple terms by Wolcott (1999), "A question such as 'What is going on here?' can only be addressed when fleshed out with enough detail to answer the related question, 'In terms of what?'" (p. 69). With this in mind, consider once again the research questions posed by Patrice in her study of families served by Early Head Start:

1. What is the meaning of infant well-being from the perspective of families who participate in Early Head Start?
2. What is the experience of families who participate in Early Head Start?

The first question addresses the need for her inquiry to reflect the focus and details of her description (the meaning of well-being, the experience of participation) as well as how she is choosing to render this description (from the perspective of families). The second question suggests a softening of her focus, broadening her depth of field so that she does not miss the place of these behaviors and meanings in context.

Such dual emphases illustrate the complementary themes contained within an ethnographic perspective: a sharp focus on the circumstances of observed behavior and a holistic breadth of vision that embraces, and works toward making explicit, the shared understandings of culture.

Phenomenology

The following summary draws upon the work of Benner (1994), Giorgi (1994, 1997), Holstein and Gubrium (1994), Moustakas (1994), Polkinghorne (1989), Ray (1994), Schutz (1967, 1970), Seidman (1998), Stewart and Mickunas (1990), and van Manen (1990). For further exploration and clarification of these ideas and concepts I encourage you to consult these sources.

The Focus and Purpose of Phenomenology

Phenomenological studies investigate the meaning of the lived experience of a small group of people from the standpoint of a concept or phenomenon. Rooted in the philosophical perspectives of Edmund Husserl (1859–1938) and subsequent philosophical discussions by Heidegger, Merleau-Ponty, and Schutz, phenomenology in its varied forms has figured prominently to influence research approaches in sociology, psychology, nursing and the health sciences, and education.[1]

---

[1] It is beyond the scope of this text to explore in depth the range of philosophical camps under the phenomenological banner. Potential users of this approach should have some knowledge of the philosophical underpinnings of what it means to study how people experience a phenomenon, looking to references such as Stewart and Mickunas (1990) as a good place to start. Researchers in education and the social sciences might be especially attentive to distinctions between *social* phenomenology (see Holstein & Gubrium, 1994; Schutz, 1967, 1970) and *psychological* phenomenology (see Giorgi 1994, 1997; Moustakas, 1994; Polkinghorne, 1989; Tesch, 1990).

Phenomenological researchers focus on what an experience means for persons who have had the experience and are able to provide a comprehensive description of it. The underlying assumption is that dialogue and reflection can reveal the *essence*— the essential, invariant structure or central underlying meaning—of some aspect of shared experience (e.g., the essential structure of a respectful interaction between parent and teacher, or the essence of being a participant in a particular program). As Polkinghorne (1989) suggests, the reader of a phenomenological study should come away with the feeling, "I understand better what it is like to experience that" (p. 46). Typically, phenomenologists generate information through long, in-depth interviews (see Seidman, 1998), augmented by critical self-reflection by the researcher.

Basic Assumptions of the Phenomenologist

- Human behavior occurs and is understandable only in the context of relationships to things, people, events, and situations.
- *Perceptions* present us with evidence of the world, not as the world is thought to be but as it is lived. Thus, understanding the everyday life of a group of people is a matter of understanding how those people perceive and act upon objects of experience.
- The reality of anything is not "out there" in an objective or detached sense, but is inextricably tied to one's consciousness of it (an idea that phenomenologists discuss in terms of the *intentionality of consciousness*). Accordingly, you cannot develop an understanding of a phenomenon apart from understanding people's experience of or with that phenomenon.
- Language is the central medium through which meaning is constructed and conveyed. Thus, the meaning of a particular aspect of experience can be revealed through dialogue and reflection.
- It is possible to understand and convey the *essence,* or central underlying meaning, of a particular concept or phenomenon as experienced by a number of individuals.

Orienting Concepts of Phenomenology

Epoché.   This refers to the ability to suspend, distance ourselves from, or "bracket" our judgments and preconceptions about the nature and essence of experiences and events in the everyday world. This is an integral part of the phenomenologist's approach: to suspend judgments about what is real until they are founded on a more certain description of how everyday life (or some aspect of it) is produced and experienced by its members. Such bracketing lies at the heart of the "phenomenological attitude" and sets that posture apart from what Schutz (1970) labeled the "natural attitude," which assumes that the world is "out there," separate and distinct from our perceptions or interpretations of it (Holstein & Gubrium, 1994). Thus, phenomenological descriptions focus not on things (what is) but on their meaning (the nature of what is).

Life-world.   The *life-world* refers to one's ordinary conscious experience of everyday life and social action. It encompasses the practical reasoning and commonsense knowledge that people take for granted. In these terms, the aim of phenomenology is to describe what the life-world consists of or, more specifically, what are the concepts and essential structures of experience that give form and meaning to the life-world (Schwandt, 1997).

The Nature of Phenomenological Questions

Phenomenological questions are targeted toward understanding the meaning of lived experience and the essence of a particular concept or phenomenon. For example, had Patrice proceeded with her study in the manner of a phenomenologist, she might have attempted to substantiate the essential structure of a caring service provider–family interaction during a home visit. (We would have to assume, as well, that her definition of problem, purposes, conceptual context, and so on had helped to establish her problem and question as best suited to a phenomenological approach.) She might then have stated her research question as follows:

> From the perspective of a parent whose family participates in Early Head Start, what is the essential structure of a caring service provider–family interaction?

or

> What is essential for the home visit experience to be described by the parent as a caring interaction?

These types of questions translate into a type of inquiry that encompasses basic tenets of a phenomenological approach:

- The researcher enters the field of perception of participants.
- The researcher sees how participants experience, live, and describe the phenomenon.
- The researcher looks for the meaning of the participants' experiences (Creswell, 1998).

Although not explicitly conveyed by either of these questions, but just as integral to a phenomenological approach, would be Patrice's commitment to set aside, or bracket, her preconceptions about the nature of the home visit experience. The only explicit assumption she might carry into this inquiry, one that she would likely address and substantiate in her conceptual context, would be to suggest that there *is* an essential structure of a caring interaction in the home visit situation. The nature and substance of that interaction would be the focus of her study.

Grounded Theory

The following summary draws upon the work of Charmaz (1990, 2000, 2002), Creswell (2002), Glaser (1978, 1992), Glaser and Strauss (1967), Strauss (1987), and Strauss and Corbin (1994, 1998). For further exploration and clarification of the following ideas, I encourage you to consult these sources.

The Focus and Purpose of Grounded Theory

The explicit aim of grounded theory is developing a substantive theory that is derived from and grounded in data. Or, if an existing theory seems appropriate but somehow inadequate relative to a topic of inquiry, then this theory may be elaborated and modified as the researcher plays additional and ongoing instances of data against it. The emphasis in grounded theory research tends to be on "process" theory—that is, theory that addresses a sequence of actions and interactions among people and events that occurs over time and that pertains to a substantive topic (Strauss & Corbin, 1998).

Forms of grounded theory research.   Grounded theory is rooted in the sociological work of Barney G. Glaser and the late Anselm L. Strauss in the 1960s. As originally conceived and reflected in their pioneering book, *The Discovery of Grounded Theory* (1967), the approach reflected basic tenets of symbolic interactionism and highlighted the authors' respective expertise in the inductive development of theory (Glaser) and qualitative field research (Strauss). In subsequent decades, differing perspectives about conducting grounded theory research, including separate tracks developed by Glaser and by Strauss, led to several dominant designs: the systematic approach associated with Strauss and Corbin (1994, 1998), the emerging approach associated with Glaser (1992), and the constructivist approach associated with Charmaz (1990, 2000, 2002). To supplement the following brief summary of distinctions, see the thorough discussions by Creswell (2002) and Babchuk (1997).

Arguably the most widely known and applied grounded theory approach, the *systematic* design of Strauss and Corbin is also the design most associated with detailed, rigorous techniques for data analysis. Prescribed procedures in the form of coding categories and subcategories, and the development of a visual diagram to present the theory thus generated, are characteristic components of this approach. A grounded theory study of this type might conclude with propositions that explain the relationships among categories contributing to the developed theory.

In a break from his earlier work with Strauss, Glaser (1992) proposed an *emerging* design that counters what he believed was Strauss and Corbin's overemphasis on a preconceived framework for categories and for theory verification rather than theory generation. Glaser's more flexible and less prescribed approach does not force theory into categories but instead focuses on connecting categories and emerging theory according to a set of criteria that includes fit, work, relevance, and modifiability (see Glaser, 1992).

Charmaz's *constructivist* approach counters what she sees as a descriptive emphasis on facts and acts in the other two designs with a more subjective emphasis on the feelings, assumptions, and meaning making of study participants. This approach also grants greater significance to the role of the researcher in the process. A constructivist study also avoids predetermined categories as might be found, for example, in Strauss and Corbin's coding scheme.

Grounded theory can be discussed in terms of certain characteristics that reflect elements of all three types of design, as suggested by Charmaz (2002) and Creswell (2002) in the list on the following page:

- Researchers study a process related to a substantive topic.
- Researchers engage in simultaneous and sequential collection and analysis of data.
- Researchers engage in an inductive construction of abstract categories, constantly comparing data with an emerging explanation or theory and refining the categories.
- Researchers integrate categories into a theoretical framework that specifies causes, conditions, and consequences of the studied process.

Common misunderstandings about grounded theory.   The term *grounded theory* is often used in a nonspecific way to refer to any approach to developing theories or concepts that somehow begins with data. This unfortunate and misleading characterization relates to a fundamental misunderstanding regarding practice. The fallacy pertains to the notion that the researcher enters a setting as a "blank slate" who gathers data and then watches theory emerge inductively from the data. In fact, the task is far from purely inferential. This complex process incorporates induction, deduction, and verification, bringing together prior theoretical commitments with emergent and evolving analytical schemes.

Basic Assumptions of the Grounded Theorist

- Human beings are purposive agents who take an active role in interpreting and responding to problematic situations rather than simply reacting to experiences and stimuli.
- Persons act on the basis of meaning, and this meaning is defined and redefined through interaction.
- Reality is negotiated between people (that is, socially constructed) and is constantly changing and evolving.
- Central to understanding the evolving nature of events is an awareness of the interrelationships among causes, conditions, and consequences.
- A theory is not the formulation of some discovered aspect of a reality that already exists "out there." Rather, theories are provisional and fallible interpretations, limited in time (historically embedded) and constantly in need of qualification.
- Generating theory and doing social research are part of the same process.

Orienting Concepts

Theory.   As described by grounded theorists Strauss and Corbin (1994), theory consists of plausible and provisional relationships that the researcher proposes among concepts and sets of concepts. The assumption is that the plausibility of a theory can be strengthened through continued research; that is, tentative theories or theoretical propositions are further explored and refined through application to additional instances of data. Researchers can aim at various levels of theory, but most grounded theorists direct their efforts toward developing *substantive* theory that stays close to the data to explain the case at hand rather than higher-level "general" or "grand" theory (see Schwandt, 1997, for further explanation of these distinctions).

In sum, two features of grounded theory are especially notable: (1) grounded theories are always traceable to the data that gave rise to them, and (2) grounded theories are fluid and provisional, demanding a reexploration of their relevance and "goodness of fit" with each new situation that emerges.

Conceptual density. Grounded theorists seek to construct theory that is *conceptually dense*—that is, a theory that contains many relationships among concepts. In contrast to the phenomenological concern for the essence or essential structure of a concept or phenomenon, for example, grounded theorists are interested in evolving patterns of action and interaction among events and happenings, and hence with capturing process analytically (Strauss & Corbin, 1998). The constructivist grounded theory approach (see Charmaz, 1990, 2000) would vary this emphasis on relationships among facts and acts to incorporate the feelings and perspectives of participants, including the researcher, as they experience and give meaning to a process.

Constant comparison.   In the process of analysis, grounded theorists employ the method of *constant comparison*. This method reflects the characteristic stance of refusal to accept a report at face value. The researcher is constantly asking not only "What is going on here?" but also "How is it different?" In this sense, it is a self-corrective process in which the researcher draws upon analysis of one set of data to guide analysis of the next set of data (Charmaz, 2000, 2002).

As summarized by Schwandt (1997), constant comparison means that the researcher looks at indicators or incidents from the data (actions, events, perspectives) for similarities and differences. From this the analyst identifies underlying uniformities in the indicators and constructs a preliminary category or concept. These categories are compared with each other and with additional indicators from the data to further define the concept. The researcher develops theories by proposing plausible relationships among concepts, and these theories are reexplored through additional instances of data. The process goes on until additional analysis no longer contributes anything new about a concept (that is, *theoretical saturation* is reached).

The Nature of Grounded Theory Questions

Research questions in grounded theory tend to reflect an interest in understanding a process or change over time. For example, had Patrice proceeded with her study as a grounded theorist, she might have focused on how some dimension of the home visitation process in Early Head Start (e.g., the nature of the family/home visitor relationship or social class differences) influenced family experiences or interactions. She might then have proposed a research question like the following:

How does the home visitation process in Early Head Start affect participants' perceptions and priorities regarding the parent-infant relationship?

Or, working with a different aim and another core concept:

> What is the influence of social class on the nature of interactions and the development of relationships between families and home visitors in the Early Head Start program?

Both questions reflect the grounded theorist's commitment to understanding the ways reality is socially constructed. And each, in its own way, sets Patrice up to remain close to her data and build categories systematically from incident to incident (e.g., home visit to home visit) and from incident to category. A category for the process addressed in the first question might turn out to be the parents' understanding of infant well-being or definition of help-seeking behavior. The second question, in particular, would orient Patrice toward tracing the influences of class differences as precisely as possible. She would also study influences flowing in the reverse direction (i.e., the impact of developing relationships on perceptions of class differences). In both cases, she would proceed with a single story line, offering a core concept and its attendant theory as a way of making sense of the data.

A Cautionary Summary

Ethnography, phenomenology, and grounded theory, if not viewed holistically as discipline-based traditions of inquiry, all run the risk of being co-opted as fashionable stores of methods and techniques in qualitative research. The caution in this summary relates to the ease of appropriating selected procedures associated with an approach—that is, selected ways of looking—but failing to realize the full meaning and potential of these procedures as part of a systematic and well-defined way of conceptualizing human behavior and social processes. As Wolcott (1999) warns in the case of ethnography, people who claim that they are doing ethnography based solely on their use of participant observation as a strategy or on their repeated but unexamined use of the term *culture* fall short of realizing their claim. So, too, with those who might claim to be doing grounded theory based solely on a characterization of their approach as inductive; or phenomenology based solely on an expressed concern for participants' perspectives.

If your conceptual components are aligned, at least provisionally, reflecting thoughtful consideration of how *problem* relates to *intent* relates to *theoretical context* relates to *question* and so on in dialectical fashion, your methodological approach should present itself as an inevitable option. This was the case with Patrice, whose eventual commitment to an ethnographic label flowed naturally and logically from her extensive conceptual groundwork and the nature of her research questions. The remaining sections in this chapter address how you might reach a similar level of commitment in your own work.

ASSESSING GOODNESS OF FIT

When and how does it matter to distinguish and declare that I am working within a particular tradition of research?

Affixing a label to your research approach means that you can situate your work within a specific set of assumptions, intentions, conceptual emphases, and disciplinary roots like those described in the previous section. It also indicates that you are confident enough to identify yourself with others engaged in similar work. This is a significant commitment: When you engage a particular research tradition, you also assume responsibility to participate in the ongoing dialogue to define it (Wolcott, 1990).

This suggests that a dose of discretion may be warranted when laying claim to a research approach. Discretion does not mean that you avoid a solid commitment but rather that you make sure your decision is informed by thoughtful consideration of the following types of issues:

- how you link question and approach
- where you focus your attention
- whether you claim the whole or borrow pieces

Linking Question and Approach

Key Consideration: *Understanding the fit between research question and approach helps you to establish your claim to a particular research tradition.*

A strong argument can be made for claiming your research approach at the point when you have a well-thought-out research question in hand. The link between research question and approach builds upon a set of fundamental propositions:

- Particular types of questions position you to look at certain aspects of reality more (or more effectively) than others do.
- Particular research approaches serve to illuminate certain aspects of reality more (or more effectively) than others do.
- Some types of questions are thus better suited to certain approaches; that is, they *position* you more effectively to see what is *illuminated*.

Some researchers claim in rather direct terms that the nature of the research question "determines" the research approach (Morse, 1994) or that the research question can be "encoded" with the language of a research tradition (Creswell, 1998). To illustrate, Morse suggests the following linkages:

- A research question focused on describing values, beliefs, and behaviors that come into play as people interact regularly suggests an ethnographic approach.

- A research question focused on the meaning of a phenomenon, particularly one that elicits the essence of experiences, directs one to a phenomenological approach.
- A research question focused on process, in the sense of understanding change or experience over time (which may entail phases or stages), feeds into a grounded theory approach.

Even if you are hesitant to reason in such direct terms, do consider the underlying logic and necessity of a good fit between question and approach. Whether or not this means your question has determined your approach, your explicit examination of the linkage between the two is a key step in affirming your decision to claim a particular research tradition.

Focusing Your Attention

Key Consideration: *Distinguishing what you are doing as associated with a particular approach matters in the sense of helping you attend to certain types of things and not others.*

Research purposes and questions enable you to approach fieldwork with a sense of what you are looking for and why that might matter. But they provide limited guidance when it comes to determining to what or whom you actually attend as you pursue your questions in the field. For additional help you can look to the orienting concerns and focus of the research tradition with which you choose to align yourself. For instance, identification with a research tradition as you enter the field enables you to shape and orient the initial query "What's going on here . . . ?" with qualifiers like the following:

". . . in terms of what I can learn from talking to individuals who have directly experienced and can describe this particular phenomenon" (phenomenology)

". . . in terms of what I can learn from attending to what some people say they are doing, what these people say they should be doing, and what I actually see them doing relative to what they have said" (ethnography)

". . . in terms of what I can learn by attempting to trace some aspect of experience over time, attending especially to how this process is made apparent through interactions between people and between actions and their consequences" (grounded theory)

Note that such qualifiers do not direct you to attend to specific people or things (e.g., "If I'm proceeding ethnographically, I need to speak with *this* person in *that* place at *this* time."). Instead they provide guidance as to the *types* of people or things toward which you should direct attention (e.g., "If I'm proceeding ethnographically, I need to speak to these types of people in these types of circumstances"). As such, they reflect your intent as an ethnographer, phenomenologist, or grounded theorist, while contributing at a practical level to decisions about where to direct your attention in the field.

Claiming the Whole or Borrowing Pieces

Key Consideration: *You should be clear about whether you are laying claim to a research tradition in its entirety or drawing upon selected aspects of it.*

Any research approach, even if embraced in its entirety, is only a broad prescription for research; you should not count on your selection of a research tradition to put your entire set of research procedures neatly into place. So, too, you should not claim to be doing phenomenology (or ethnography or grounded theory) if all you are doing is employing specific and selected techniques from the phenomenological (or ethnographic or grounded theory) storehouse of procedures.

At times it can appear difficult to identify studies that are the exclusive or "pure" expression of a particular research tradition. It is often easier (and more accurate) to claim that studies are only relatively more oriented toward this or that tradition. In the case of my own doctoral research, which I labeled an "anthropological life history," I claimed to be using life history as an approach within an ethnographically oriented study of an experienced teacher's adjustment to a new school and community context. The complementary features of ethnography's detailed observation of behavior in a naturalistic setting and life history's retrospective reconstruction of an individual's life resulted in something less than "pure" anything, but significantly more than a convenient or attractive pairing of perspectives. There is certainly nothing wrong, and potentially everything right, with this type of blending, so long as you are clear about how and when each research approach is informing your decisions about what is worth knowing and how you are applying that knowledge.

To that end, you need to be attentive to the types of distinctions and assumptions discussed earlier (see "Distinguishing among Options"). You also need to keep in mind that (a) being well-versed in a research tradition, and (b) feeling the need to follow its every tenet to the letter are different matters (Wolcott, 1990). My contribution as an ethnographer to my dissertation study did not demand the level of immersion, contextualization, cultural interpretation, and so on that would enable me to claim that I was doing *an* ethnography. That I was sufficiently oriented along ethnographic lines to situate my life history work within a cultural frame of reference did support my claim to be doing a "good" study, appropriate to the research aims and questions I had posed. That more than satisfied my (and my committee's) claims-making needs.

SUMMARY

You need to have more practical and compelling reasons for deciding upon a particular type of qualitative research than the appeal of a label. This chapter focused on clarifying the reasons that underlie when and how it matters to declare that you are working within a particular tradition of research.

Just as there is no one way to see the world, there is no such thing as *the* approach to a problem identified for inquiry. Ethnography, phenomenology, and grounded theory illustrate three distinct ways, among many other options, for *seeing* (reflecting perspective and intent) and *looking at* (reflecting methods and procedures) a problem or topic as a qualitatively oriented researcher. This chapter has cautioned against appropriating selected procedures associated with an approach—that is, selected ways of looking—without grasping the full meaning of these procedures as part of a systematic, well-defined, and discipline-based way of approaching inquiry.

Questions of when and how it matters to declare that you are working within a particular research tradition encompass issues of the fit between question and approach, the way you focus your attention, and your decision to claim the whole or only parts of a tradition. The fact that these issues were not addressed until this chapter reinforces the premise that methodological decisions are based on prior considerations of problem, purpose, perspective, and the questions that you pose.

PART TWO

ANTICIPATING YOUR INQUIRY
IN ACTION

When Patrice sat down with faculty members on her dissertation committee to discuss and initially defend her proposed research on the participation of families in Early Head Start, questions arose around the role she envisioned for herself "in the field." Given her experience as an early childhood educator and home visitor for early intervention programs for more than two decades, concerns naturally turned toward how the substantial professional knowledge she would be bringing to her interactions might affect her research aims. The following dialogue is an excerpt from that meeting.

"So, Patrice, if you happen to be conducting fieldwork in a household when the mother puts the baby to bed with a bottle of Kool-Aid or sugar water, are you going to say anything? Or what if one of the parents is a smoker, and the baby is constantly inhaling secondary smoke? Are you going to offer any comments?"

Patrice considered her response carefully. "Initially, I expect, I will name such episodes in my fieldnotes and explore their implications in my field journal. The families, of course, will know that I have worked as a home visitor, but I will be a researcher from the get-go, and my goal will be to learn from them."

"Yes, but you will be changing over time, as will your relationships with these families, so you may eventually do more than simply name these instances," suggested Bruce, a committee member.

"Absolutely," interjected John. "You cannot avoid the fact that, with your presence and your expressed interest, you are in a very genuine sense joining the circle of care around these infants and these families. And you will be bringing more than 14 years' worth of professional experience and knowledge to the setting, not to mention your own insights as a parent."

"I'm not going to pretend to know 'nothing,'" offered Patrice. She paused to consider her next response. "But I also realize that, up to this point, I have given more attention to my role as participant observer than I have to my role as interventionist, and it is critical that I pay attention *to the experience of interventionist as participant observer. As John said, I am joining the circle of care around the participant families, and I do want to align with them."*

"What does that mean—'align with them'—in terms of your dual role as researcher and practitioner?" asked Mary Jane, also an early childhood educator.

"Well, I'm not sure yet if I actually envision myself as having that dual role in this case," responded Patrice. "However, I do know that to enhance my understanding of the influence I exert on the family context in which I am present, I will have to be sensitive to and track instances where I am aware of my own interventions, intentional or not . . . I will have to monitor my interventionist self."

GETTING INTO PLACE

In raising hypothetical scenarios about Kool-Aid and parental smoking, Patrice's committee member foreshadowed moments in her fieldwork when she might have to play out her research aims against possibilities for professional or personal intervention. How would Patrice balance what she knows, what she needs to know, and what she wants to know when interacting with others as a fieldworker? How might her concerns about what could be or what should be affect her decision to share something openly with her study participants or keep it to herself? Patrice's response and the ensuing discussion direct attention to a key challenge associated with getting into place as a fieldworker, namely, how to portray oneself and one's purposes to participants in the setting (Rossman & Rallis, 1998).

Portrayal of involvement is just one of many practical and ethical concerns that researchers must address before and during their engagement in a field setting (see Chapter 8). Generally speaking, positioning yourself as a fieldworker entails not only how you get to, get around, and conduct yourself in a particular setting—the physical, procedural, and mechanical aspects of being in the field—but also what your intentions and questions are as you go about it. "Being there" is a prerequisite for conducting field-based inquiry, but ultimately, it is your intent, not your presence, that makes fieldwork what it is (Wolcott, 1995).

The chapters in Part One considered this matter of intent, addressing what it is that brings you to the point of fieldwork in the first place. Time now, in Part Two, to consider how you situate yourself to learn whatever it is you want to learn.

MAKING GOOD USE OF OPPORTUNITIES

Fieldwork is largely a matter of recognizing what might be learned as situations present themselves. As a theory of how your inquiry should proceed, this statement no doubt lacks the specifics you are seeking as you anticipate your own efforts in the field. It does, however, suggest an eminently practical way to direct your thinking as a fieldworker concerned with strategy. In *The Art of Fieldwork* (1995), Harry Wolcott states,

The element of strategy turns on two complementary questions to be reviewed over and over:

- Am I making good use of the opportunity before me to learn what I set out to learn?
- Does what I have set out to learn, or to learn about, make good use of the opportunity presenting itself? (p. 90)

Chapters 7 and 8 maintain a steady focus on both questions, mirroring Wolcott's advice to keep concerns of strategy in mind as you attempt to observe and experience what you are interested in observing and experiencing. These two chapters also advance Part One's central theme of orchestrating connections, highlighting in particular the intrinsic link between *substance* (what the fieldworker finds out) and *method* (how the fieldworker finds it out) (Emerson, Fretz, & Shaw, 1995). Together, the chapters move through considerations of approaching and anticipating fieldwork decisions and strategies.

Strategic Considerations for Fieldwork

Chapter 7 suggests strategies for selecting and justifying how you as a fieldworker will collect and generate data, highlighting strategic considerations prior to fieldwork.

Establishing Your Inquiry's Integrity

Chapter 8 addresses practical and ethical considerations involved in establishing the credibility and integrity of your study.

Writing Your Proposal

Chapter 9 addresses the ways in which discrete aspects of the conceptualization process find expression as you shift from efforts to establish the logic and coherence of your inquiry (Chapters 2–8) to the presentation and justification of your study in the form of a written proposal.

STRATEGIC CONSIDERATIONS FOR FIELDWORK

How does fieldwork serve the aims of my inquiry? What are the key strategic and relational issues I need to consider as I approach fieldwork? What judgments underlie my decision to go about fieldwork in a particular way?

The overarching theme for this chapter and Chapter 8 might best be conveyed by the cautionary phrase, "Look carefully before you leap into fieldwork." Taking a cue from Wolcott's complementary questions in the introduction to Part Two, are you in place—conceptually, methodologically, and ethically—to make good use of fieldwork to serve your inquiry? And does "the field" that lies before you make sense as the place where your inquiry can and should play out?

As you address these questions (over and over), take a second helpful cue from Clifford Geertz's time-honored observation that it is "not necessary to know everything in order to understand something" (1973, p. 20). Even if that seems self-evident, it is crucial to keep in mind the ease with which being in the field invites you to consider everything going on about you, while also suggesting that the something you are after is to be found wholly through the methods and techniques of fieldwork. It can feel wonderfully affirming to finally be out there in the field, but it is deceptively so if you neglect to precede fieldwork with a thorough questioning of why and how it serves the aims of your inquiry.

This chapter addresses a number of critical issues that can help you determine whether what you want to accomplish is most effectively accomplished through fieldwork. And if fieldwork is the way to go, what should factor into your decision to go about it in a particular way? These strategic considerations will help you find that *something* in the *everything* of the field.

The following strategic considerations come together under six conceptual headings, a set of fundamental issues that address whether you are *in* place as well as in the *right* place to pursue field-based inquiry: intent, focus, involvement, familiarity, positioning, and role awareness. Each of these, respectively, feeds into secondary considerations of need, purposefulness, role portrayal, sense making, context, and topic sensitivity (Figure 7.1).

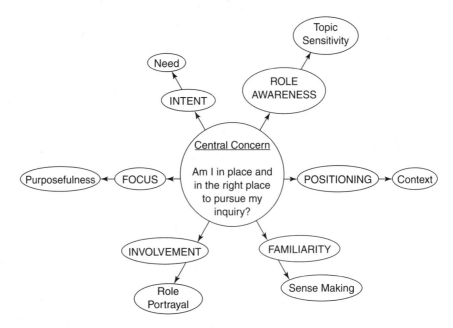

Figure 7.1
Strategic Considerations for Fieldwork

INTENT

With *intent* we revisit a basic premise emphasized in the introduction to Part Two: Simply "being in the field" is not enough to make what you are doing fieldwork; your intent makes it so. Doing fieldwork, or simply borrowing a fieldwork technique or two, must serve your research aims, and a fundamental criterion for evaluating your decision to pursue fieldwork is whether, as you proceed, you are moving closer to accomplishing those aims.

This criterion may seem obvious, but it is important to consider that fieldwork can be a remarkably inefficient way simply to gather factual data that, for example, a skilled survey researcher could generate in a more timely and less labor-intensive manner. Intent thus feeds into the secondary consideration of *need,* as you determine whether, and how efficiently, fieldwork will give you what you need, all the while keeping in mind that it may be more than you need to pursue your research question (Figure 7.2).

To illustrate, a number of years ago I was involved in a cross-disciplinary research project that teamed qualitative researchers like myself with mathematics educators in developing descriptive case studies of 12 school sites throughout the United States. The project was designed to portray the complexity of changing mathematics teaching and learning by describing the efforts of schools as they implemented their particular visions of what school mathematics should be (Ferrini-Mundy & Schram, 1997).

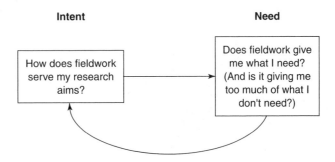

Figure 7.2
Fieldwork and Intent

During an early planning session involving all the project documenters, one memorable exchange between two team members over the nature and extent of fieldwork that was required for the study revealed significant differences in their interpretation of the project's aims. One researcher clearly tended to look intensively, but seldom more than once, at a phenomenon, embodying in her stance the structure and economy of research aimed at limiting or reducing the variables of study. The other favored a contextual and holistic emphasis that meant looking again and again at a site in order to capture both its ordinariness and its variety. Research aims for the first tended to be derived, whether explicitly or implicitly, from the question, "How can mathematics instruction be improved?" For the second, the central aim was embedded in the question, "Why is mathematics teaching occurring this way in this setting?" The first sought consistency across contexts; the second expected variety within and across settings. Each reflected a distinct intent and a different level of need for fieldwork.

Intent is what makes the difference between (a) simply putting yourself out there in the field and (b) using fieldwork to take you somewhere consistent with your research aims. The worth of fieldwork *as fieldwork* is assessed by the basic question: Is this experience giving me what I need (or, conversely, is it giving me too much of what I don't need) to pursue my research question? As Wolcott (1995) cautions, if you feel that fieldwork is getting *in* your way rather than helping you *make* your way, reconsider your decision to pursue it, or at least to pursue it in the manner in which you have initially approached it.

FOCUS

Attention to research aims in the context of fieldwork also demands renewed consideration of the important distinction between the *focus* and *locus* of your inquiry. Chapter 2 discussed the significance of this distinction in terms of helping to clarify the purposes of your inquiry. My intent here is not to repeat that line of reasoning but to underscore the need to put your study's focus—its driving, conceptual concerns—back on the front burner now that you are actually going to have contact

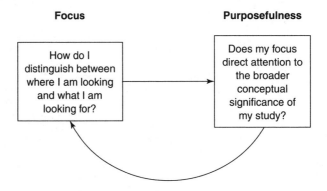

Figure 7.3
Fieldwork and Focus

with your research phenomenon. It is at this juncture when the temptation to confuse where you are looking with what you are looking for returns as an immediate,
tangible concern.

Attending to the focus/locus distinction in a meaningful way means that you
continually return to the question "What's at issue here?" and systematically revisit
your research aims. If you find yourself continually falling back on the feeling that
"there must be something intrinsically valuable about this place," then your fieldwork may already have become a data-driven activity in which you have traded res-
olution, or focus, for scope (Seidel, 1992).

Focus thus feeds into the secondary consideration of *purposefulness,* as you
monitor the ongoing relevance and emerging significance of your original aims relative to actual events bounded by time, space, and circumstance (Figure 7.3). This
is part of the necessary mindwork that carries fieldwork beyond the reactive experience of moving your body around an interesting place and taking in what is offered and toward a more proactive stance of sustained, intentional inquiry.

INVOLVEMENT

The concept of *involvement* takes us back to the types of practical and ethical questions raised in the discussion of Patrice's research that prefaced Part Two. How
might your perceptions of what is, and your feelings about what could be or should
be, affect your decision to share something openly with study participants or keep
it to yourself? How much do you share with study participants about your aims as
a researcher?

Getting into place as a fieldworker, as Dolby (2000) reminds us, is more a social
than a physical enterprise, an ongoing process of negotiating competing knowledge
claims and moral positions, through which you locate yourself as a participant at
some level in a setting (Rogers & Swadener, 1999). As a fieldworker, you will be
caught up in how a place is represented to you. In turn, those whose experiences

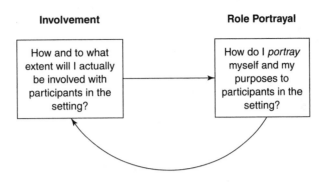

Figure 7.4
Fieldwork and Involvement

you are attempting to understand will be sorting through how you are representing yourself and your purposes in being there. This dual consideration of degree of involvement and portrayal of involvement is illustrated in Figure 7.4.

Degree of Involvement

As framed by Rossman and Rallis (1998), these two aspects of a fieldworker's intended involvement suggest movement along different continua of participation and openness. Degree of participation is characterized at one end of the continuum as being fully present as a human researcher, what Rossman and Rallis term "coparticipation." This level of participation, more than simply being immersed in a setting, entails the active collaboration of setting participants in shaping the agenda for inquiry, for example, by making observations, suggesting changes, and creating different avenues of questioning (Rogers & Swadener, 1999).

At the other end of the continuum, participation refers to the researcher being present as an engaged spectator who is experiencing, but is not overtly involved in, what is happening around him or her. Like Rossman and Rallis (1998), I believe all field-based researchers are, to varying extents, participants in settings. Consistent with this perspective, I, too, do not devote attention to the question of whether one is a participant observer or a nonparticipant observer. Sitting behind a two-way mirror and watching toddlers in a child-care facility, for example, is more accurately labeled laboratory work, not fieldwork. However, step into the room of children, even as a passive (but visible) observer, and you become a participant, at least in the sense that your presence and immediate responses have the potential to impact the natural behavior and activity of those in the room.

In between on the continuum are varied degrees of *immersion*—that is, "both being with other people to see how they respond to events as they happen and experiencing for oneself these events and the circumstances that give rise to them" (Emerson, Fretz, & Shaw, 1995, p. 2). This is accomplished through learning what is required to become a member of the participants' world, and approximating their experiences (by following local standards for behavior, moral conduct, and so on), but not actually becoming a member of that world (Emerson et al., 1995). Practical and ethical implications of partial engagement in a setting will factor into the discussion of trustworthiness in Chapter 8.

Several basic premises affect your role as a researcher regardless of where you locate yourself on this continuum of participation:

- Your participation on the continuum can, and probably will, change over the course of your inquiry. (Remember Bruce's advice to Patrice in the vignette that introduced Part Two.)
- Different degrees of participation can either help or hinder data collection; more participation does not necessarily facilitate your efforts, though it often does. (Here again, check to see if your level of participation is consistent with your research aims.)
- Amount of participation is a factor of time in the field; more involvement requires more time. (And more time and involvement likely translate into greater familiarity and trust between the researcher and participants in the setting.)

Portrayal of Involvement

Portrayal of involvement, according to Rossman and Rallis (1998), invites a twofold consideration: how to portray yourself and how to portray your research purposes to study participants. A basic concern in your code of ethics as a researcher is that people must be informed of who you are and what you want. One extreme of the continuum—in which your role as researcher is covert, participants do not know that research is being done, and you provide false explanations (or none at all) about why you are there—is an ethical violation and these days is simply not acceptable. Acceptable portrayal of involvement ranges on a continuum from complete openness (participants know that research is going on and that you are doing it) and full explanation (participants are fully informed about the study's purposes) to partial sharing or being "truthful, but vague" (Taylor & Bogdan, 1984, p. 25).

When might you choose not to disclose fully your specific aims as a researcher? The answer turns on both ethical and pragmatic concerns. Foremost among these is the researcher's judgment that participants' awareness of details might make them particularly self-conscious. The core concern is that, if participants were aware of the specific research focus, they might adjust their behavior and actions to fit their understanding of the researcher's purposes and expectations.

For example, although she was conceptually focused on implicit class issues associated with providing services to families impacted by poverty, Patrice chose to convey her aims to participants in terms of understanding the experiences of families *in general* served by Early Head Start. She did not want to draw undue attention to a characterization ("being poor") that might hold entirely different meanings to study participants. If she turned poverty (or any topic) prematurely or inaccurately into a sensitive issue, she risked transforming her research agenda into something of a self-fulfilling prophecy (see the related discussion of role awareness later in this section).

We will revisit relational issues and ethical dilemmas tied to informing others of one's research purposes in the discussion of trustworthiness in Chapter 8.

FAMILIARITY

The concept of *familiarity* also returns us to some of the basic concerns raised in the vignette that introduces Part Two. These concerns spin off of considerations of involvement. When interacting with others as a fieldworker, how do you balance what you know, what you need to know, and what you want to know? How do you create opportunities to have your preconceptions—what you thought you knew—disrupted by new information?

If we follow Patrice further down the path of inquiry to her preparations for fieldwork, it becomes apparent that the key challenge posed by familiarity was the ease with which she could become her own informant even before she entered the field. For example, in anticipation of questions that she might ask an Early Head Start home visitor in a preliminary interview, Patrice drafted the following, among others:

> What happens to families when they sign up for Early Head Start?
> How is an "ap" handled?

Both questions reveal Patrice's prior experiential knowledge regarding how Early Head Start works from the perspective of those who administer it. The first question, embedded with the assumption that families simply "sign up" for the program, risks leap-frogging over the potentially complex dynamics of making contact (do the families always take the first step?) or how and why it comes about that families seek services (or that the services seek the families) in the first place.

The second question, also assumption-bound, carries an added risk for Patrice. In using "in-house" slang ("ap," for application), Patrice may inadvertently convey to the person she is interviewing that she is already "up to speed" on the processes involved in administering program services. That may suggest to the interviewee that it is all right to skip over other, seemingly insignificant, but potentially valuable, parts of his or her explanation.

Like the example of Tim and the assumptions underlying his initial research questions in Chapter 5, here is a consequence of the familiar being all too familiar. Patrice needed to anticipate this prior to entering the field and plan accordingly. Her best strategy in this regard was to make sure that the questions she planned to ask were not framed in terms of the way she already saw things. Instead, her questions should be set up as opportunities, or openings, for her vision of things to be discounted (whether or not it actually ends up being discounted). For this to occur, her questions need to be free from preconceptions and, at least initially, more open-ended. For example:

> How is it that families and Early Head Start come to be linked up?
> What needs to happen for this to occur?

Once you actually enter the field, familiarity will feed into the related consideration of *sense making,* as you work to maintain the important distinction between what you see or experience and what you infer or assume about an experience (Figure 7.5).

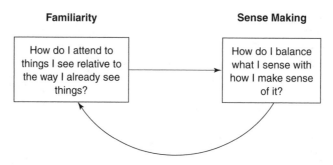

Figure 7.5
Fieldwork and Familiarity

POSITIONING

Positioning refers to the fact that you are working to get into place not only to gather but also to generate data. As suggested in Chapter 1, features that count in a setting do not simply announce themselves as significant and wait to be collected. Given some set of intentions and some frame of reference, you must see and make sense of what is to be seen. The operating assumption, as introduced in Chapter 3, is one of coherence: there is a way of thinking and seeing, a context for what's going on, in terms of which the information you gather will make sense in a particular way. Prior to actual fieldwork, you need to consider how you are situated to get the information (gather data) and then put the information in context (generate more data), as suggested in Figure 7.6.

A key element in considering this process is to recognize that behind every exploration made or question asked, there needs to be some sort of working hypothesis (Wolcott, 1995). By working hypothesis I mean an informed sense of potential significance, an assumption of coherence, that sets you up for more than gathering data simply for the sake of gathering data. As a qualitative researcher, you are not out to formalize or disprove hypotheses, but neither are you in the business of picking up data in anticipation that an answer to your question is somewhere in the pile. The overarching theme of this chapter establishes itself more firmly and precisely: Look (think, check your reasoning) before you leap (ask, impose).

For Patrice, consideration of her positioning played into her decision to spend her first several months of fieldwork "peering broadly" at the overall dimensions of Early Head Start's home visitor program as a means to "nest" her subsequent and more extensive engagement with the families. This was no mere toss of the coin ("Well, I guess I'll talk to the home visitors first, then the families"). It was an approach Patrice determined to position her in time and circumstance relative to specific sources and types of data and based on the consideration that her research aims were best served if certain (context-heavy) information preceded other (nitty-gritty) information.

It is also important to keep in mind that the twofold task of gathering and generating data is in most cases *your* problem. You are the one trying to become com-

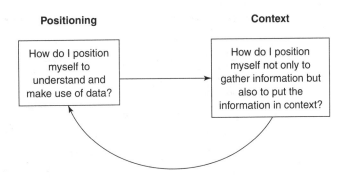

Figure 7.6
Fieldwork and Positioning

petent enough to question and then figure out how things connect with each other and to a big picture. Things will continue to fit together for participants in the setting whether you are there or not and regardless of whether and how you make sense of it all.

At the same time, you will be in a setting doing something—observing, asking, documenting—that is not naturally or normally done there. Your sensitivity to the imposition of a research agenda onto the setting, even when accomplished under the most collaborative or coparticipatory of terms, plays into the sixth and final strategic consideration discussed here, role awareness.

ROLE AWARENESS

"In the simple act of *asking*," writes Wolcott (1995), "the fieldworker makes a 180-degree shift from observer to interlocutor, intruding into the scene by imposing onto the agenda what he or she wants to know" (p. 102). This is a deliberate shift, and as such, it is something you should anticipate and plan for prior to entering the field. Informed anticipation builds upon:

- awareness of role ("As a fieldworker, I know that sometimes I will simply be taking in whatever happens to come along; at other times, I will be making my personal and research preferences known").
- consideration of implications ("In the former role, the agenda is laid before me and I can be nondirective; in the latter role, I take charge of the agenda").

The play of shifting roles feeds into consideration of *topic sensitivity* ("How much do I want to reveal of the fact that some issues or topics are of more consequence than others in my inquiry?"), as suggested in Figure 7.7. The inherent challenge, as Wolcott (1995) suggests in building upon his earlier statement, is distinguishing between what you would like to know and how to go about making

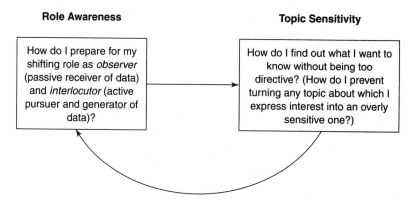

Figure 7.7
Fieldwork and Role Awareness

that interest known. Managing this distinction, which often turns on a split-second decision to ask a question or hold it for later, is not something for which you can explicitly plan. It does require that you bring to fieldwork the awareness that your role is not constant. You must understand that shifts in your role have implications for how, and how much, you influence the direction of your inquiry.

SUMMARY

Entering the field as a researcher reflects a deliberate choice informed by thoughtful consideration of the following question:

Are you in the right place strategically to pursue a field-based inquiry?

This chapter addressed considerations involved in determining your response to this question. Especially critical is researcher intent and whether the anticipated fieldwork is consistent with what is needed to accomplish research aims. This underscores your responsibility to revisit continually the question, "What's at issue here?" and to avoid the temptation to confuse where you are looking (locus) with what you are looking for (focus).

Getting into place as a fieldworker also entails consideration of how involved you plan to be in the setting and how you intend to portray that involvement. Questions of involvement may or may not entail risks posed by familiarity with the setting. That is, the more familiar you are with a situation, the greater the risk that your preconceptions will unduly influence what you see and experience, and how you make sense of it all. Degree and portrayal of involvement necessarily play into your shifting roles in the field and how you go about making your research interests known to study participants.

CHAPTER 8

ESTABLISHING YOUR INQUIRY'S INTEGRITY

What can I do to ensure the credibility of my study, not only with respect to other researchers, policy makers, and practitioners, but also in the eyes of the study's participants? How do I maintain the integrity of my study, both methodologically and ethically?

This chapter prepares you to respond to the practical and ethical issues involved in establishing the *trustworthiness* of your study. This is the point at which the intellectual and conceptual coherence discussed in Chapters 3 and 4 is brought to bear on the overall integrity of your inquiry, as judged by standards for competent practice and ethical conduct (Rossman & Rallis, 1998).

How can you demonstrate that you and your account can be trusted, that you have the interests of your study's participants at heart, that you conduct your research ethically and with sensitivity to the politics of the topic and setting? These questions alert us to two necessary—and necessarily intertwined—dimensions of trustworthiness that contribute to your study's integrity. The first dimension, addressed in the following section as *practical considerations,* pertains to standards for competent performance as a fieldworker and reflects upon issues of researcher presence, the inevitable selectivity of fieldwork, and the play of subjectivity. The second dimension, *ethical considerations,* refers to standards for conduct based on moral principles and includes issues of posturing and role presentation, exchange and disclosure, and consequences of making public the private.

PRACTICAL CONSIDERATIONS

As a researcher you will face legitimate questions from readers and potential beneficiaries of your study that focus on the accuracy or plausibility of what you report and claim, how you generated the findings, and whether (and to whom) the study is useful. Rossman and Rallis (1998) describe these concerns in terms of a study's truth value, its rigor, and its significance or applicability. The challenges and dilemmas that overlap these concerns translate into several practical considerations you need to address as you seek to establish the integrity of your research. These considerations include presence, selectivity, and subjectivity (see Figure 8.1).

The first critical step is to make explicit the nature and implications of these concerns prior to entering the field. By doing so at this point I seek to establish them

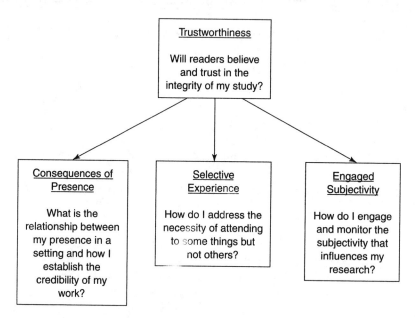

Figure 8.1
Practical Considerations in Establishing Trustworthiness

not as problems, but as perspectives that can help me proceed with my inquiry—and you with yours—in a competent and credible fashion.

Consequences of Presence

What is the relationship between my presence in a setting and how I establish the credibility of my work?

The implications of "being there" and "seeing for myself" reflect in varying ways upon the truth value of one's work. This statement in no way asserts a direct relationship between presence and credibility. Being in a setting or interacting with people does not in itself provide the compelling authority for a credible account, given that the fieldworker's experience of that setting or with those people at best approximates rather than replicates participants' experiences (Bittner, 1988; Emerson et al., 1995). Patrice, for example, set for herself the task of engaging in the lives of families served by Early Head Start but did not (and could not) experience directly the day-to-day exigencies of membership in such a family.

It is inevitable, however, that a researcher's presence in a setting has implications for what takes place and how events are given meaning. Early on, Patrice expressed concerns that her presence might be viewed as a potentially contaminating influence on how participants talked or behaved ("They're going to say things because they think that's what I want or need to hear"). This type of influence, referred to as "reactivity" (Maxwell, 1996) or "consequential presence" (Emerson et al., 1995), implies that fieldworker presence is a disruption or defect to be controlled or eliminated.

An alternative perspective suggests that relationships between field researchers and those in the setting help to reveal the underlying terms and bases on which processes and events occur. Proponents of this view claim that one's sustained presence can contribute to a fieldworker's heightened sensitivity to subtle understandings—for example, how meanings emerge through talk and action and how perspectives change over time—that are not readily available through detached or highly controlled observation or interview methods alone.

Rather than cast your understanding of presence one way or the other and hope for the best, recognize and harness what is fundamental to both perspectives: the inherent connection between what you come up with and how you go about doing it (Emerson et al., 1995). This means you come to terms with what you can and cannot accomplish as a researcher working within boundaries of time and circumstance. In terms of process, it means recognizing the necessarily interpretive nature of what you construct in the field.

Both aspects of fieldwork, practical constraints and interpretive necessity, turn on the same logic. Start with the practical. Whether observing, interviewing, experiencing, or pursuing some combination of strategies, you cannot be everywhere at once or take in every possible viewpoint at the same time. Instead, in conjunction with those in the setting, you develop certain perspectives by engaging in some activities or talking to certain people rather than others. Inevitably, whether by chance, deliberate choice, or the following of "political fault lines" in the setting, you are exposed to differing priorities and perspectives (Emerson et al., 1995). As a result, your task is not to assume there is one "natural" or "right" perception that determines "the truth," but to uncover any number of possible truths or meanings manifested in the experiences or words of participants (Mishler, 1979). You build assertions toward the never-quite-attainable goal of "getting it right," approximating realities but not establishing absolutes.

Your task, both derived from and constrained by your presence, is thus inherently interpretive and incomplete. The bottom line is that there is no bottom line: It is not necessary (or feasible) to reach some ultimate truth in order for your study to be credible and useful. To claim that something you have documented or described "rings true" is not incompatible with a recognition that your judgment or interpretation of it may be wrong or "off" a bit (Hammersley, 1990). Credibility does not demand certainty. This becomes more apparent as we consider the play of selectivity in the fieldwork experience.

Selective Experience

How do I address the necessity of attending to some things but not others?

It follows from our discussion of presence that qualitative fieldworkers cannot view their task simply as a matter of gathering or generating "facts" about "what happened." Nor can they too readily take one person's version of what happened, or what is important, as the "complete" or "correct" version of these matters. Rather, fieldworkers engage in an active process of interpretation and selection: noting some things as significant, noting but ignoring others as not significant, and missing other potentially significant things altogether (Emerson et al., 1995).

Addressing the necessity of attending to some things but not others filters down to questions of purpose. For example, if Patrice is going to describe a meeting between a home service provider and a family, it will make a considerable difference whether her interest is in socioeconomic differences revealed in the encounter, whose agenda is directing conversation, or how the immediate setting is influencing behavior, for example. Were Patrice to develop descriptions based on each of these various interests, they might overlap considerably, but they might also vary enough to suggest different meetings altogether.

That multiple descriptions of the same event are possible should not be construed as a challenge to the credibility of an account. The point is that each description needs to be an accurate or plausible representation of the phenomenon to which it refers (Hammersley, 1990; Schwandt, 1997) and that this representation accurately reflects the purposes and sensitivities of the researcher. Describing the same event for different purposes does not lessen the need to support one's findings with evidence or to establish that the evidence for your findings is more plausible and convincing than the evidence for alternative findings (Schwandt, 1997).

To claim that qualitative fieldwork is distinctively a matter of selective experience, then, is to acknowledge the practical necessity of reducing (not replicating) the lived complexity of social life. But choosing what to attend to is not a process of sampling according to some predetermined principle. Rather, selectivity is

- *purposeful,* reflecting fieldworkers' need to attend to how their purposes, particular values, and biases influence the conduct and conclusions of the study.
- *circumstantial,* reflecting fieldworkers' understanding of findings as contingent upon the particular circumstances under which they elicit or construct them (and consequently reflecting the expectation that the findings cannot be absolute and unchanging).
- *intuitive,* reflecting fieldworkers' changing sense of what might possibly be important to a developing interpretation and what might be interesting or useful to readers of the study.
- *empathetic,* reflecting fieldworkers' sense of what is important or useful to study participants.[1]

All of these qualities feed directly into what is perhaps the most insistently present consideration of trustworthiness discussed in this section—how subjectivity plays out in the conduct of research.

---

[1]Further discussion of these and related ideas can be found in Creswell & Miller, 2000; Emerson et al., 1995; Glesne, 1999; Richardson, 1994.

Engaged Subjectivity

How do I engage and monitor the subjectivity that influences my research?

"The inescapable fact of our presence in research," write Jansen and Peshkin (1992), "means that we are present to make choices. Choices equal subjectivity at work" (p. 721). Although some of your choices about what to attend to and how to interpret it may be consciously made, others derive from personal qualities that come into play prior to and through your interactions with events and people in the field. This is the play of subjectivity.

At issue is the question of how and to what extent personal qualities or attributes, such as emotions or personal sensibilities, influence, or should influence, the research process (Jansen & Peshkin, 1992). Or, as Behar (1996) suggests more directly, how do you make the most of your own emotional involvement with the material?

For Patrice, this issue first took shape as an insight into the virtues of rigorous self-reflection as she took her early "reconnaissance" steps into the field. During some coding of preliminary data she noted:

> I have discovered that continuing to make sense of myself is a necessary part of the research . . . looking closely at the self who produces a document at a moment in time and thinking about how that self at that moment was constructed . . . taking the step of reflecting on my range of responses, thoughts, feelings recorded in my fieldnotes, my process journal, my memos. For example, "What had I read/heard/experienced that made me write that?"

The point is to suggest that aspects of the self can serve as important filters through which one perceives the topic or phenomena being researched. This does not mean you establish the goodness or rightness of your account in some private or personal sense. To the contrary, when you deliberately engage and monitor your subjectivity, you use your feelings and emotional responses as authentic points of departure, or cues, for inquiring into why you are perceiving and to what effect you are interpreting matters as you are (Glesne, 1999; LeCompte, Schensul, Weeks, & Singer, 1999; Peshkin, 1988).

Such a cue occurred for Patrice during one of the first times she accompanied an Early Head Start home visitor to the house of a family enrolled in the program. She noted in her field journal her surprise and discomfort as she observed the home visitor sit at a table with the family in adult-focused activity, with the child on the periphery. This contrasted sharply with her own early intervention experiences in the years prior to her research, when home visits consisted of sitting on the floor with the child in child-focused activity, with the adults on the periphery. Patrice noted her emotional response not as a judgment on what she was observing, but as a cue that prompted her to reexamine some of her assumptions and shape new questions regarding the context and dynamics of home visits. She actively sought in subsequent fieldwork to see what she was not seeing, to detect, for example, if more could or should be made of how and why people position themselves as they do during home visits.

Seen in this more "virtuous" light (Peshkin, 1985), subjectivity becomes something to capitalize on rather than to discipline or exorcise, a means to enhance not distort the credibility of your study. In practical terms offered by Glesne (1999, p. 105):

> It is when you feel angry, irritable, gleeful, excited, or sad that you can be sure that your subjectivity is at work. The goal is to explore such feelings to learn what they are telling you about who you are in relationship to what you are learning and to what you may be keeping yourself from learning.

This goal—and, in particular, its dual focus on what you are learning and what you may be keeping yourself from learning—serves well to guide your consideration of subjectivity. A logical extension of this understanding is the idea that the subjectivities that influence the course of research are not those of the researcher alone but also of study participants, an idea conveyed by the term *intersubjectivity*. An implication of this for the trustworthiness of your interpretation lies in the potential for the values, attitudes, and perspectives of both researcher and participants to be changed through the research process (Glesne, 1999). For now, we have taken the first step, making explicit the nature and implications of these concerns prior to entering the field.

ETHICAL CONSIDERATIONS

In the process of negotiating relationships in the field, how quickly I have come to understand my position as one of privilege! It is so highly privileged because of the personal and delicate information I have that has the potential to harm relationships.

Patrice, Reconnaissance Report I, July 2001

Ethical considerations are inseparable from your interactions with study participants in the field. Although ethical decisions are certainly not peculiar to qualitative inquiry, the negotiated and heavily contextualized nature of ethical dilemmas is a defining characteristic of qualitative fieldwork. In this section I address three key considerations in establishing the trustworthiness of your inquiry from an ethical standpoint:

- posturing and role presentation
- disclosure and exchange
- making public the private

As in the previous section, my goal is to convey the nature and implications of these concerns as a means to anticipate and frame dilemmas, not necessarily to resolve them. My guiding questions adjust the focus on trustworthiness to reflect integrity in the particular context of relationships with study participants (see Figure 8.2).

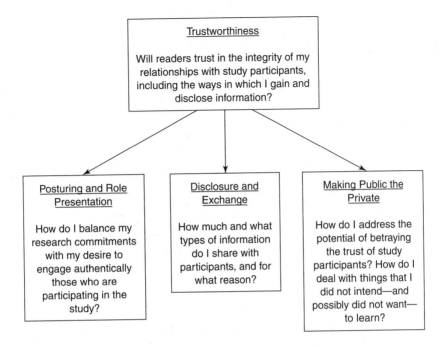

Figure 8.2
Ethical Considerations in Establishing Trustworthiness

Posturing and Role Presentation

How do I balance my research commitments with my desire to engage authentically those who are participating in the study?

A foremost consideration in establishing fieldwork relationships is your ability to maintain the distinct intentionalities embodied in your role as (take your pick) participant observer, resident visitor, friendly stranger, detached confidant, or neutral advocate, among others. Even under the most collaborative of circumstances with study participants, you and they are walking together on separate paths. Your dual responsibility as a researcher—to engage (walk together) with others while remaining faithful to the primary aim of conducting research—is a pairing of intentions separate from participants' everyday lives, although you hope they will understand and support your efforts.

Impression management (how you present yourself) or *posturing* thus becomes critical to the types and the integrity of relationships that you form in the field. The most commonly faced ethical decisions in this regard tend not to be about whether you present yourself in a false or affected way (posturing in a deliberately misleading and thus morally unacceptable sense). Rather, the key predicament lies in when and how you present and play out the genuine, multiple roles that you bring to the field (posturing in a strategic sense).

A month or so after the initial meeting with her committee members to discuss her research, Patrice faced this predicament head-on. She reflected on the questions raised during that meeting about the potentially conflicting expectations inherent in her current role as a researcher among families and her longtime professional role as a family interventionist. Recalling the specific question about observing a parent place Kool-Aid in her infant's bottle (see Part Two's introductory vignette), Patrice commented:

> *I undoubtedly will have an intervening effect on the families through my modeling of behavior and interactions. There is an arrogant assumption here, reflecting my professional interventionist self, that families might see in my actions the "right" way to do things. As a participant observer, I don't want families to copy me! This is why I first responded to the question about the Kool-Aid in the neutral way that I did. Now I think I would respond to the situation by explaining to the parent why a doctor or Early Head Start says not to put Kool-Aid in the infant's bottle. This might be slipping into my non-researcher professional role, but I see it more as a way to avoid saying what I personally would do. I don't want to be seen as the person who knows what is "right."*

Intimate interactions like this hypothetical one around an infant's care pose ethical challenges for fieldworkers and suggest the heavy burden placed on them to express personal opinions, to act less like passive observers, and to expose their "true" selves. There are no easy answers to help you deal with such pressures. But it is crucial that, in your actions, you maintain the distinction between being something or someone you are not—generally regarded as an unethical ploy—and doing what comes naturally and seems appropriate to fit in and benefit your research aims. Consider Patrice's decision to dress a certain way for her fieldwork among families served by Early Head Start:

> *I have taken the designer label off the old, used backpack I carry. I bought white canvas sneakers at Wal-Mart (since my old sneakers say Adidas on the back) and . . . will go without a watch if I see few families wearing watches. When I go places with families, I want to try to fit in as much as possible with them. I envision joining the "circle of care" not as an interventionist, but as a free ride to town, as an extra set of hands when it's time to get food stamps or something like that.*

Patrice's considerations reflect the range of intentions that, in varying degrees of emphasis, feed into a researcher's ongoing and ever-changing presentation of self in the field. These include:

- *rapport building,* or a process of establishing trust with participants that primarily serves the needs of the researcher; intention and purpose reside with the researcher. Fieldworkers manage their appearance and behavior in order to foster continual access to information (Glesne, 1989).

- *friendship developing,* or the seeking of relationships founded on mutual af-fection and goodwill; friendship participants are equal actors in establishing, maintaining, and defining the duration, need, and ends of their relationship. "Friendship may bias data collection; but it may also contribute an even more potent voice than that gained through rapport" (Glesne, 1989, p. 53).
- *boundary spanning,* or developing relationships that transcend differences between groups or individuals within a setting, a need that is implied by the researcher's move from being strictly a passive observer to an active participant. Regarded by some as a form of cultural brokering (Goetz & LeCompte, 1984), boundary spanning often places the fieldworker in the delicate position of having to explain one group's actions to another, while avoiding being "marked" as an advocate for a particular group or perspective (Deyhle, Hess, & LeCompte, 1992).

The emergence of bias in developing friendships can pose particular challenges. Glesne (1989) describes three ways that friendship seems to bias one's inquiry. First, the researcher may unconsciously be tempted to talk primarily with persons he or she likes or finds politically sympathetic. Second, the researcher, although con-sciously aware of people who might be the best sources of information, may be de-nied access to them because of his or her friendship with others in the setting. Third, friends of the researcher in the setting may over-identify and, in so doing, act or re-spond in ways that they think the researcher wants them to act or respond. Glesne concludes, "The case for cultivating research friendships under considered circum-stances remains open, but, as a rule, I think we should give priority to developing and maintaining rapport, not friendships" (p. 50).

Conventional wisdom cautions fieldworkers to remain as neutral as possible, which in practical terms means paying attention to the assumptions underlying your relation-ships with others. Foremost among these is that you, as researcher, are shaping rela-tionships largely according to the research needs you bring to the setting. Your intent introduces into "what's going on" the trust-building, distance-reducing, disclosure-demanding process that fieldwork entails. How this plays out with respect to what re-searcher and participants ask and expect of each other is the next ethical consideration.

Disclosure and Exchange

How much and what types of information do I share with participants, and for what reasons?

A defining characteristic of relationships with fieldwork participants, in contrast to those with survey or questionnaire respondents or treatment groups, is the degree of personal disclosure that is both permitted and necessitated on the part of those involved (Deyhle et al., 1992). Tensions and dilemmas naturally emerge from the ef-fort required to balance the level of shared knowledge necessary to establish rap-port and the sense of responsibility that accompanies earned trust.

Your success as a fieldworker depends on being able to make requests of others. Typically, your requests (for information, for time, or simply to be present) fall outside the normal flow of events and must be negotiated and judged by participants to be appropriate or fair. This gives rise to a recurring ethical issue: How much information should you share in order to get the information you need from others? Ask yourself:

- Am I deceiving participants or putting them at risk if I deny them a complete account of my purposes? If people know fully or precisely what I am looking at or looking for, and why, will they be as forthcoming as I need them to be?
- How much should I tell participants about my preliminary sense of problem or conceptual context—that is, what I think may be going on?
- Should I let participants know in the (likely) event that my questions and focus of attention shift during the course of the study?

The answer that qualitative researchers would likely offer to any of these questions rests on a general concern to ensure that participants behave and respond in the most natural and genuine way possible. But implied in each case is the idea that the exchange of information in fieldwork unavoidably carries the potential for deception—not necessarily to the unethical extent of lying, stealing, or breaking promises, but deception nonetheless.

These two unlikely bedfellows, genuineness and deception, are linked by a pragmatic, mutually justifying logic that arguably addresses the needs of both researcher and participants. That is, to the extent that researchers' partial or calculated sharing of information gains them a fair representation of participants' natural behavior or understandings, their portrayal of them is accordingly more authentic and credible (Emerson et al., 1995; Peshkin, 1984; Punch, 1994). In short, the decision to withhold is made to acquire more valid data, not to confuse or harm.

When I began fieldwork for my research into the learning and participation of Laotian students in a small high school (Schram, 1993, 1994), I initially told those in the setting that I wanted to understand the experiences of students in the school, and nothing more. I spoke truthfully but not fully about my intentions, basing my partial disclosure on a desire to ensure that participants acted and responded as naturally as possible.

Pair this logic with the pragmatic position that some "dissimulation is intrinsic to social life, and, therefore, also to fieldwork" (Punch, 1994, p. 91), and you have a pragmatic rationalization acceptable to some researchers (though certainly not a badge of honor they wear on their sleeves). But you still find yourself in a discomforting, delicate, and ethically challenging position, one that clearly favors (or *privileges,* to use a popular term these days) researcher needs and control of the relationship.

What is clear is that ethical standards and requirements of informed consent, avoidance of harm, and confidentiality are opposed to outright deception. Such standards make clear that it is unethical for researchers to:

- misrepresent their identity to gain entry into settings otherwise denied to them.
- deliberately misrepresent the purpose of their research.

- break promises made to people or otherwise act in ways that leave participants feeling cheated or put at risk (Glesne, 1999; Punch, 1994).

The principle of *informed consent* forms the basis of what is required by university human subject review committees for each dissertation and research proposal. This is typically addressed by means of an informed consent form or letter with the following components (adapted from Rossman & Rallis, 1998): (a) the researcher informs participants as fully as possible about the study's purpose and audience, (b) participants are provided with enough information so that they understand what their agreement to participate entails, (c) participants give that consent willingly (and indicate so with their signature), and (d) participants understand that they may withdraw from the study at any time without prejudice or penalty.

And so you make your case for disclosure, honoring the trust on which your access to information is predicated and building on considerations of "doing good," not simply avoiding doing wrong. The call today for collaborative or participatory research encompasses the possibility that "collaboration in labor" contributes in unique fashion to establishing trust between researcher and participant, to greater mutuality in the interpretation of findings, and to more equalized power in research relationships (Zigo, 2001). This continues to be a promising approach to ethical responsibilities in research. But collaborative or otherwise, your challenge in initiating and sustaining the inquiry process is the same: convincing participants (as well as yourself) that the research is good and worthwhile, all the while making and honoring requests that jostle the balance of openness and trust.

Making Public the Private

How do I address the potential of betraying the trust of study participants? How do I deal with things that I did not intend—and possibly did not want—to learn?

Among the many implications of conducting oneself ethically as a fieldworker is the need to balance the requisites of gaining access and trust with the obligation to attend responsibly to the revelation and public sharing of knowledge that accompanies your eventual departure. With the access that participants grant you to trusted and privileged information and observations of unguarded behavior come the concerns about what you should disclose, at what cost, and for what audiences. Anticipation of this responsibility should inform every step you take toward and within the field.

The dialectic that informs much qualitative fieldwork—that is, unexpectedly acquired knowledge suggesting previously unforeseen questions leading to new directions for inquiry—heightens the risk of being misunderstood. For example, your attempt to reformulate an inadequate question based on feedback from the field—in your eyes a means for improving the credibility of your study—may be construed by participants as changing topics in midstream in violation of a prior understanding. Or, in another twist on unintentional learnings, you may (and likely will) discover more than you want to learn, either in the form of information that is potentially dangerous to some people or that may be interesting but not of critical importance to your study. What to do?

Wolcott's (1995) advice to be candid but discreet in deciding what you report reflects the wisdom of always having in mind clear boundaries for your inquiry. The following guidelines highlight this point and provide a helpful summary of considerations to guide your conduct in the field (adapted from Rossman & Rallis, 1998; Wolcott, 1995; Zigo, 2001).

- Let participants know but also periodically remind them why you are there (either directly or, for example, by keeping your documenting activities and paraphernalia conspicuous).
- Remain aware of the boundaries you have established to define your purpose and focus so that you can convey those boundaries to participants. At the same time, be clear with participants about your need to remain flexible and open to the possibility that your focus will be refined or redirected.
- Set up opportunities to discuss fully the relative boundaries of power among all participants, recognizing and accepting the elusiveness of full equality in even the most well-intentioned partnerships.
- Be clear about your motivations and intentions when engaging with participants in activities that are, or that appear to be, other than for research purposes. Fieldwork does not preclude such shared and purposeful engagement (for example, babysitting children so the mother can attend to errands). At the same time, participants will justifiably feel betrayed if knowledge gained under such circumstances is used to inform a published or otherwise shared account.
- Help participants maintain some sense of the nature and scope of what you intend to report (for example, by commending participant statements that are particularly helpful, or informing a participant that a remark he or she just made is clearly outside the range of the study).

In sum, attending responsibly to the manner in which you structure and sustain your relationships with study participants obligates you to act in ways that treat those relationships as ends as well as means (Rossman & Rallis, 1998). In part, this means behaving as you would want everyone else to behave in a given situation (with respect and dignity) and, conversely, not doing anything to others that you would not want them to do to you (e.g., exploit relationships or make promises you cannot keep).

It also means following through with the assumption that you can and will do some good with what you have come to know. Patrice's research will not bring guarantees of infant well-being and greater equity to families served by Early Head Start; nor can she promise lifelong personal friendships to participants in her study. At the least, however, she can ensure that she will write honestly and cogently about what she has worked hard to understand, share the knowledge that she has gained in a responsible and respectful fashion, and incorporate what she has learned into her own professional conduct.

Experienced fieldworkers readily note that a researcher is apt to receive more good from his or her research—status, attention, income—than study participants (Glesne, 1999; Rogers & Swadener, 1999; Wolcott, 1995). This is often unavoidable but not unethical, unless of course the researcher's concern fastens exclusively on personal gain. As conveyed in Patrice's prefacing statement to this section on ethical considerations, conducting fieldwork represents an assumption of privilege that researchers need to acknowledge (Emihovich, 1999). With that acknowledgment comes the obligation to attend responsibly to the ethical stance of not exploiting any person in any circumstances.

SUMMARY

Entering the field as a researcher reflects a deliberate choice informed by thoughtful consideration of the following questions:

- Are you prepared to respond to practical questions about the trustworthiness of your fieldwork?
- Are you in place ethically to do right by study participants?

This chapter introduced issues that affect the trustworthiness, or overall integrity, of your study. Key issues that define practical aspects of trustworthiness include:

- the influence of researcher presence, highlighting the link between what you come up with and how you go about doing it.
- the inherent selectivity of qualitative fieldwork, highlighting the task of reducing (not replicating) lived experience.
- the play of researcher subjectivity, highlighting the need to attend to how aspects of the self may be helping you to learn—or keeping you from learning—certain things.

Key issues that define ethical aspects of trustworthiness include:

- posturing and role presentation, highlighting your dual responsibility to engage participants authentically while remaining faithful to your aim of conducting research.
- disclosure and exchange, emphasizing tensions that emerge from the uneasy balance between the level of shared knowledge necessary to establish rapport and the sense of responsibility that accompanies earned trust.
- making public the private, focusing on the consequences of revelation and, in particular, the risk that some participants may feel misunderstood or even betrayed by what a study reveals.

CHAPTER 9

WRITING YOUR PROPOSAL

How do I transition from conceptualizing to proposing a study? How do I convey to others that my study is worthwhile and that I am capable of conducting it? How do I use features of my conceptualization to inform and shape the structure of my proposal? What actually goes into my research proposal?

This final chapter offers some practical guidelines and advice on how to make the shift from conceptualizing your inquiry to proposing a study. My less explicit (but no less important) aim is to ensure that you understand the important distinctions between these two tasks. Overall, if you have done a thorough and thoughtful job on the conceptualizing end of things, you will find that crafting a proposal is the far easier task of the two.

FROM CONCEPTUALIZING TO PROPOSING

A research proposal represents the point at which you present and justify your research ideas in a manner that takes into account others' (a faculty committee's or funding agency's) collective judgment about what constitutes a coherent and worthwhile study. This is a decisive shift from all that you have been doing up to this point. You are stepping out of a process characterized by relative independence of judgment and an exploratory mind-set that enabled you to tack creatively between focus and breadth, observation and intuition, theory and Theory. Now you must consider how to reduce the iterative and interactive process in which you have been engaged into a product—a document—that others can understand and value.

Viewed in this manner, your proposal highlights the decisions you have made to determine and justify the *what, why,* and *how* of your inquiry (Marshall & Rossman, 1999). "Each piece of your proposal," writes Maxwell (1996), "should be a clear answer to a salient question about your study" (p. 102). A well-conceived proposal includes attention to some form of the following questions (adapted from Marshall & Rossman, 1999; Piantanida & Garman, 1999; Rossman & Rallis, 1998):

- What is the focus of your inquiry?
- What are the aims of your inquiry?
- How and why is your inquiry worthwhile and important?
- Does the way you plan to proceed with your inquiry make sense?

- Is it clear that you know what you're up to in conducting the inquiry?
- Is there an overall coherence to the reasoning that underlies your inquiry?

In transitioning from conceptualizing to proposing, you adjust your aims. The emphasis now is on presentation, not discovery; communication, not just coming to terms. Figure 9.1, which I will explain more extensively in the section on "Structuring Your Proposal," portrays the processes and products that inform and distinguish these two tasks.

ARGUING FOR YOUR STUDY

Rather than provide a merely descriptive specification of what you will do, a qualitative proposal should present a clear, contestable argument that explains and justifies the logic of your study (Maxwell, 1996; Piantanida & Garman, 1999). In a manner not unlike the generative and selective process that characterized the construction of your conceptual context (Chapter 4), you now make the case for the coherence, feasibility, and relevance of your inquiry in its entirety. The selective aspect of the process stands front and center in that your task at this point is one of getting down to essentials: how each choice you have made flows logically into others, and how all fit together as a coherent whole. Maxwell (1996) offers perhaps the best and most pointed advice I have encountered on this issue:

> Your proposal should be about *your study,* not the literature, your research topic, or research methods in general. You should ruthlessly edit out anything in the proposal that does not directly contribute to the explanation and justification of your study. (p. 101)

Here again it is helpful to revisit some of the cautions and pivotal concerns noted in Chapter 4's discussion of how to develop a conceptual context. Now, as then, you do not want to replace the formative task of arguing for your study with a thinly veiled summative effort to convey how learned you have become in the process of conceptualizing and constructing it. (A tedious and comprehensive display of your theoretical, methodological, and/or political savvy is *not* how to demonstrate that you are capable of conducting your research.) Instead, continue to emphatically embrace pivotal concepts like the following:

- **Ownership.**   Bear in mind Maxwell's advice to keep your proposal a matter of *your* study. Make sure the concepts and theories upon which you draw are serving your purposes and not the other way around.
- **Focus.**   Stay directly and meaningfully engaged with your problem and purpose. Draw upon relevant and supplementary information on a "when-and-as-needed" basis (Wolcott, 2001) rather than on a "see-how-much-I-know" basis.
- **Purposefulness.**   Do not confuse the clarity and definition you seek in a proposal with the deceptive ease of a neat, tidy, and potentially self-fulfilling explanation. You need not (and should not) avoid all that wonderful complexity with which you've come to terms, but you do need to be

CONCEPTUALIZING	PROPOSING
Problem finding & entry-level theorizing	**Title** • Contains conceptual points of reference • Orients and tracks your perspective
Situating your problem	
Clarifying practical and personal purposes	**Introduction** • Orients readers to purpose of your inquiry • Provides preview of research questions & type of study • Begins to frame the inquiry
Clarifying research purposes	
Clarifying your intellectual orientation and moral stance	**Conceptual Context and Theoretical Orientation** • Clarifies relevance & significance of your inquiry • Gives readers a clear sense of your theoretical approach • Establishes a basis for your research question
Constructing a conceptual context	
Forming and justifying research questions	**Research Questions** • Clarifies focus and logic of your research questions
Clarifying and claiming a mode of inquiry	**Research Procedures** • Provides rationalization for methodological decisions and chosen mode(s) of inquiry • Explains and justifies particular strategies and methods • Addresses practical aspects of credibility & ethical considerations
Anticipating fieldwork strategies & procedures	
Establishing practical & ethical integrity	
	Significance and Implications • Addresses "so what?" questions regarding your proposed inquiry • Reaffirms your purposes • Clarifies your claims
	Appendixes • Timetable for research • Tentative outline of chapters • Consent forms, IRB approval

Figure 9.1
From Conceptualization to Proposal

purposeful, particularly in terms of building your argument toward a meaningful and well-defined research question.

STRUCTURING YOUR PROPOSAL

A proposal requires structure. In this case, the term *structure* refers to the interrelation of parts and how their relative positioning contributes to the shape and substance of the whole. This understanding does not necessitate a rigid framework or formulaic outline, but it does encompass the need for clear definition and cohesiveness.

The proposal format outlined on the right side of Figure 9.1 and detailed in the following sections is certainly not the only way to structure a proposal, but it does reflect features generally regarded as consistent with the nature and design of a qualitative study. Figures 9.2 through 9.7, in conjunction with supplementary examples, will help to unpack and clarify the connections between these features and the conceptualizing tasks in which you have engaged thus far.

Title

Key Concerns: Conceptual Significance, Perspective

Focus and Purpose of the Title

The title of your proposal deserves careful consideration. It conveys, if not the conceptual essence, at least conceptual points of reference for your study. Some researchers claim that each word in the title should relate to a key concept in your study, adding that each concept should then be explained in the proposal's text (Piantanida & Garman, 1999). Whether or not you push your title-building efforts to this level of precision, the basic message is that the title should flag what is under study and foreshadow the perspective that is orienting your approach to the topic. To this end, you will draw most substantially on your prior work in constructing a conceptual context and clarifying your intellectual orientation as a researcher (see Figure 9.2).

Another criterion for an effective title might include whether it conveys sufficient information to catch the attention of possible readers and to enable your work to be cataloged in an appropriate category based on the title alone (Wolcott, 2001). Example 9.1 provides commentary on these issues for Patrice's study of families who participated in Early Head Start. The commentary in this example also addresses the relative merits of incorporating the context of your study and even the mode of inquiry into the title.

The Title as a Vehicle for Continuous Reflection

Example 9.1 alerts us to the *ongoing* role of the title in the development and conduct of your inquiry. If systematically monitored and reflected upon as the focus and direction of your study evolves, your changing titles can become a means to track the evolution of your perspective as a researcher. Peshkin (1985) championed this idea, noting that as researchers become increasingly immersed in what they are doing and discovering, they necessarily contend with different issues that compete for

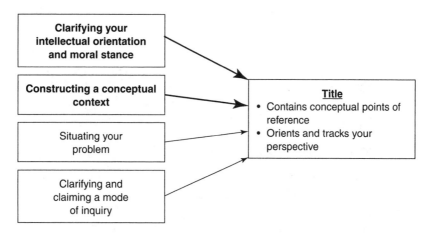

Figure 9.2
Constructing a Title

EXAMPLE 9.1   CONSTRUCTING A TITLE FOR YOUR STUDY

Patrice began developing a title for her study long before her proposal was in place, in order to track changes in her thinking during the initial phases of conceptualizing her study and, as suggested by Peshkin (1985), throughout her ensuing fieldwork. The following titles, with comments, are selected for illustrative purposes from nearly 20 titles drafted by Patrice over a 3-year period from her initial conceptualizing work to her proposal, and extending to the time of this writing, when she was still engaged in fieldwork.

December 1999 (during Patrice's early attempts to situate her problem):

"Mary, Mary, Quite Contrary, How Does Your Garden Grow?: Infant Well-Being from the Perspectives of Families Impacted by Poverty"

Patrice's Reflection: Although I intend to critique the role of Early Head Start in the lives of family participants as part of my research, the overriding question for me is how families who live in poverty view infant well-being. My hunch is that families who live in poverty have different contexts, that theirs is not one of "silver bells and cockle shells and pretty maids all in a row" [the line that follows "Mary, Mary, quite contrary. . . " in the old nursery rhyme]. I recognize the power of context and maintain that the contexts of infants being reared in poverty are misunderstood by home visitors enlisted to help their families.

Author's Commentary: Notice that, even at this early stage, this title contains a key conceptual concern of Patrice's study, namely, *infant well-being.* "Families impacted by poverty" suggests, albeit rather vaguely, the *context* in which her inquiry was starting to take shape. "Mary, Mary, Quite Contrary. . . ," aside from being an attempt at a "catchy" title, reflects some preliminary positioning around a critical perspective

---

EXAMPLE 9.1   *continued*

---

and, specifically, Patrice's stance that federal programs like Early Head Start, despite their stated intentions, actually serve to perpetuate class and power relationships in U.S. society. The subtitle starts to hint at Patrice's methodological inclination to engage these families directly and understand matters from *their* perspectives, angling her toward the potential of an ethnographic approach.

March 2001 (Patrice's proposal title):

"Infant Well-Being and the Participation of Families in Early Head Start"

Author's Commentary: Patrice did not write a reflection on this title, as she did with her others, focused as she was at the time on her proposal write-up. Several features are worth noting, for either their presence or absence in this draft. First, and perhaps foremost, this title contains the two key conceptual concerns that orient Patrice's study and that find expression in her central research questions: infant well-being and the experience of families in Early Head Start. With this title Patrice clearly identifies what is at issue in her study. "Participation of families in Early Head Start" also serves to alert us to the specific context in which her inquiry is embedded. Absent from this title are indications as to research perspective or mode of inquiry, either of which might foreshadow the nature of the portrayal that Patrice aims to generate. The absence of such features results in a clearly focused but rather neutral title—not necessarily a bad strategy at the proposal stage, when you might be feeling cautious about claims making.

**September 2001 (when Patrice shifted from preliminary
to full-time fieldwork):**

*"Helping Those Who Help Themselves: Families and Home Visitors
in Early Head Start"*

Patrice's Reflection: In some of my initial interviews with home visitors I asked the question, "What is a good family?" I asked that because I had heard home visitors saying things like, "Oh, they're a *good* family!" . . . I think that I may find that . . . what makes certain families "good" is that they are willing to help themselves and work hard to improve their condition, which are cultural characteristics borne deep within us. . . . Home visitors reinforce the Horatio Alger work ethic in families, as part of the unwritten program creed and as part of their own personal values. So this is my hunch: In order to have effective helping relationships, regardless of differences between help giver and help receiver, there needs to be the *desire* to be helped on the part of the families, and families need to show evidence of their *work* at helping themselves, which is consistent with the help giver's own understanding of what *work* is.

Author's Commentary: The key shift from the earlier title is that Patrice has replaced identification of her two guiding conceptual concerns with a much more specific notion, "Helping those who help themselves," that foreshadows what may emerge as a central theme of her interpretation. This signals a significant insight on Patrice's part and puts in place a sense of perspective on what she intends to portray. Tak-

---

EXAMPLE 9.1   *continued*

---

ing a stand with a title like this at the proposal stage would probably not work, since, by necessity, it builds upon evidence from the data. Prior to actual fieldwork, such a title would reflect merely what Patrice, in situating her problem and building a conceptual context, might *think* is going on in the setting. The subtitle works well to identify the context, though not the conceptual focus, of the study.

December 20, 2001 (over halfway through fieldwork):

"Inside Out: Infant Well-Being and the Experience of Families in Early Head Start"

Patrice's Reflection: For now I am going with "Inside Out" because that is how I explain to others what I am doing in my study. I am coming to know families with infants who participate in Early Head Start from the inside out (as an informed research friend) rather than from the outside in, which is how helping professionals typically come to know families. I am also getting "inside" the home visitors and the visitor-family relationship. Once inside, I will turn it to the outside for others to see, hopefully uncovering cultural assumptions as I go. In the process of completing the research, I have also turned myself inside out in an attempt to heighten my consciousness about how I am acting as a participant observer and how I am interpreting my data.

Author's Commentary: This holds great promise in that it incorporates many of the features of an effective title. With this title Patrice has returned to the key conceptual concerns of her study, handily phrased to also convey the specific context in which these concerns are embedded. "Inside Out," if understood in the multifaceted way described by Patrice, alerts us to matters of researcher perspective and mode of inquiry. Granted, we cannot assume that readers will grasp all that Patrice hopes to convey within those two simple words, but the title certainly holds the potential to convey, in subtle but "catchy" fashion, a sense of what Patrice is up to. This title could have served well at the time of Patrice's proposal, suggesting a less neutral (or at least a more interesting and informed) stance than expressed in that earlier draft.

"center stage" in their thinking. These issues, as illustrated in Example 9.1, may be conveyed through one's title. In effect, your title drafts serve as a way to monitor and highlight systematically your emerging insights as a researcher.

Introduction

Key Concerns: Purpose, Preview, Personal Connection

Focus and Purpose of the Introduction

The Introduction section of your research proposal serves several major purposes. First, it orients readers to the purpose of your inquiry. Second, it provides a brief preview of your main research questions and the kind of study you are proposing. Third, it begins to frame your study by explaining what has led you to focus on the

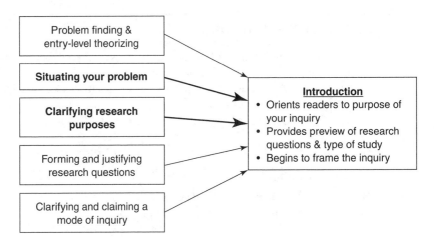

Figure 9.3
Crafting an Introduction

topic of your inquiry, conveying a personal and overall sense of its context and significance. A number of prior conceptualizing tasks, most prominently those of situating your problem and clarifying your research purposes, feed into the crafting of the Introduction (Figure 9.3).

In the example that follows, Patrice crafted the first paragraph of her Introduction with an eye toward *purpose* and *preview:*

> *This proposed research is an anthropological field study of families who participate in an Early Head Start Program. I come to this study with two questions: What is the meaning of infant well-being from the perspective of families who participate in Early Head Start, and what is the experience of families who participate in Early Head Start? I ask the questions in this way because my broader goal is to understand the complexity of the social context of infants who are growing up in poverty and to understand the home visiting relationship when families receive support services. Of particular interest to me is what happens when a middle-class home visitor meets a low-income family in the home visiting relationship.*

In this introductory paragraph, Patrice clearly and succinctly presents the purpose of her study in conjunction with a preview of her main research questions. Her opening sentence conveys in general terms the kind of study she will undertake. She wastes no words in getting to the point of her inquiry, effectively forestalling that most humbling of reader queries: "*Why* am I reading all this stuff?"

Full details and discussion surrounding research questions, the conceptual or theoretical context, and research procedures are best left for subsequent sections of the proposal (as detailed in the following portions of this chapter). A fuller presentation and justification of research questions, in particular, is most effectively placed *after* the context section of your proposal, when you have laid out the conceptual and theoretical underpinnings of your inquiry (Maxwell, 1996). This is not a hard and fast rule, but as discussed earlier, this placement more accurately represents the thinking that actually went into the formation of your questions. More importantly, it enables you to build a case that supports the logic and rationale for your questions.

As for the rest of your Introduction, which normally ranges from two to four double-spaced pages, use it to frame your study with an explanation of what has led you to focus on the topic of your inquiry, conveying a personal *and* overall sense of its context and significance. The following section, supplemented by Example 9.2, describes one way to approach this task.

Addressing Personal Context in the Introduction

Piantanida and Garman (1999) suggest that providing contextual background from a personal perspective can be an effective way to help frame your study in the Introduction. They propose two questions you might address: "What brought me to this study?" and "Why do I find it compelling?" Preliminary memos that you developed during your initial efforts at problem finding and entry-level theorizing can directly and logically feed into this portion of your Introduction.

For her Introduction, Patrice made the decision to clarify the focus of her inquiry in relation to her personal experience and context, reflecting a practice that is increasingly the norm (but is certainly not a requirement) in qualitative research proposals. As illustrated in Example 9.2, she began to address her personal connections to the topic in the second paragraph of her Introduction, eventually (but only briefly at this point) extending these connections into broader areas of concern.

EXAMPLE 9.2 ADDRESSING PERSONAL CONTEXT IN THE INTRODUCTION

The following excerpt from Patrice's proposal begins with the second paragraph of her Introduction. Her opening paragraph, as already noted, oriented readers to the nature and purpose of her inquiry and provided a brief preview of her guiding research questions. She then continued:

My questions are prompted by my experience as a home visitor in early intervention for families with infants and toddlers with developmental delays and disabilities. Many of the families with whom I have partnered are socially and economically different from myself, and I question how these differences may implicitly impede the home visiting partnership and how my understanding of infant well-being may be different from families who live in circumstances entirely different from my own.

In my privileged role as a home visitor for early intervention programs, I became a part of the lives of many families with diverse goals and priorities for their children in a range of contexts. I often felt comfortable in social and economic settings similar to that of my own childhood and my own parenting experience, and it was easier to relate to families who had a similar interaction style and who shared goals and priorities for their

---

EXAMPLE 9.2   *continued*

---

children like my own. It was the feeling of distance and disconnection, however, that intrigued me about my relationships with families who lived in circumstances different from my own. How could I support the father of a newborn infant and a toddler, both with fetal alcohol syndrome, whose alcoholic girlfriend (and the children's mother) had recently died from alcohol poisoning? What are the priorities of a family who are perpetually homeless when their goals do not seem to include housing? How could I emotionally connect with and be effective with families whose circumstances were outside my realm of experience?

The current literature on infant development, although supported by increasing amounts of cross-cultural research, does not reflect a notion of infant well-being that takes into account the social and economic diversity of our society. Professionals in the field of infant development apply concepts of emotional health and development that have been created outside the social and economic contexts of the families to whom they are often applied. This is particularly evident in the process of determining eligibility for human service programs such as early intervention.

Patrice's second paragraph directs us to the experiential roots of her research questions and provides further definition of her research purposes. In the following paragraph, she begins to uncover the personal significance of her inquiry. Her narrative foreshadows broader concerns like the play of social and economic difference within relationships, while conveying the personal relevance of her inquiry through several very specific questions arising out of her own experience. Some of her statements are drawn directly from memos she had crafted in earlier phases of conceptualizing her inquiry (see Chapters 2 and 3).

Note that Patrice's final paragraph shifts from the personal realm to establish a link between her immediate interests and broader discussions in the literature and elsewhere. Piantanida and Garman (1999) remind us that such "conceptual bridgework" is necessary when starting with an account of one's personal engagement in the topic in order to avoid the risk of appearing naïve or unduly concerned with oneself at the expense of the bigger picture being addressed. Patrice's single paragraph is informative and serves the purpose of hinting at issues to be addressed in later sections of the proposal. Others might prefer to add more about the broader context within the Introduction, drawing further on information that fed into their initial efforts to situate the problem (see Chapter 2).

What, Why, Who, Where, When, and How

The approach described in the preceding section worked well in Patrice's case, but different studies will require different amounts of information to orient readers to the purpose of a study. If we examine the entirety of Patrice's Introduction, it is apparent that she has addressed the *what, why,* and, in a general sense, the *who* of her study.

At some point, readers will need a straightforward accounting that details key procedural and contextual issues, including the setting (where), participants (who), timeline for research (when), and specifics regarding the research approach (the nitty-gritty of the how, unpacking her general claim to be conducting an "anthropological field study"). Most of these details are properly addressed in a Research Procedures section of the proposal. You should revisit the *why* of your study in a later Significance and Implications section by extending into the broader arena of research and practice some of the "conceptual bridging" (see Example 9.2) touched upon in your Introduction.

In sum, the Introduction should draw readers into your inquiry while orienting them in general terms to its nature and purpose. Its focus is appropriately on the *what* and *why* of your study. Keep in mind that you are merely setting the stage for explaining and justifying your research. It is sufficient that your audience members have a sense of what might appear on that stage, not be required to read the entire script, assured that details and dialogue will follow.

Conceptual Context and Theoretical Orientation

Key Concerns: Coherence, Relevance, Orientation

Focus and Purpose of the Conceptual Context and Theoretical Orientation

Your task as you consider this section is driven by the same question that guided your earlier efforts at constructing a conceptual context (see Chapter 4 and Figure 9.4):

> What do I need by way of theory—or, more modestly, by way of concepts—to help me develop a sound argument for what I am doing, how I am going about it, and what I am choosing to attend to in my fieldwork?

Labeling both conceptual context *and* theoretical orientation as complementary components lets you establish a level of emphasis for each with which you are most comfortable. As discussed in Chapter 4, thinking in terms of a conceptual context for your study allows you to be relatively modest when making claims about the ideas you are weaving into your work, while also inviting consideration of how these ideas *may* fit into some broader theoretical scheme. And as Wolcott (1999) notes, "we tend to be more forgiving of concepts than of theory" (p. 99).

The fundamental assumption remains that of coherence, as introduced in Chapter 4. Now, as then, you are constructing a way of thinking and seeing, an

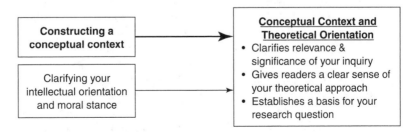

Figure 9.4
Constructing a Conceptual Context and Theoretical Orientation

orientation, in terms of which your inquiry and your reasons for pursuing it make sense. In basic terms, you are setting up the reader to understand how and why your research questions are the appropriate questions to be asking.

This means that you must establish the conceptual territory (not the entire landscape) in which your research is justified and makes sense. The focal point for this task is your prior work in formulating a conceptual argument for your inquiry in terms of *currents of thought* and the *meaningful conceptual linkages* between those currents and the topic you are proposing to study. If you have done a thorough job of "wrapping up" this earlier conceptual context work, your job at this point is essentially one of reframing or reducing that earlier argument in order to present it to an audience of others. Two helpful questions in this regard are those posed by Wolcott (2001) in describing the "tightening up" process in one's writing:

- Do you have everything you need?
- Conversely, do you need everything you have?

Example 9.3 uses excerpts from Patrice's Conceptual Context section to portray the balance one seeks between situating the inquiry within an accumulating body of knowledge and making the case for orienting your inquiry along particular conceptual and/or theoretical lines. In general, the length of this section varies considerably among students, depending on the nature of the topic and the complexity of concepts requiring definition. It seems reasonable to expect that a sound conceptual argument can be made in 15 or so pages. The key is staying focused: Are you engaging directly with your problem by drawing on the relevant work of others on a "when-and-as-needed" basis (Wolcott, 2001, p. 74), or are you parading everything you can find on your topic?

The "Lit Review" Issue

This last question alerts us to a secondary assumption at play in this section of your proposal, also mirroring your previous context work: the need for your efforts to be generative and selective, rather than simply summative and descriptive. As before, you should think in terms of composing an argument, not presenting a review. To help position yourself for this task, revisit Chapter 4's discussion of pivotal concerns in developing a conceptual context (pp. 44–45), and particularly the guiding questions aligned with the authority, focus, ownership, and purposefulness of your writing.

In highlighting these pivotal concerns, I am not seeking to put you at odds with a faculty committee that may demand a traditional, comprehensive "review of the literature." At the same time, experience suggests that expectations for the "lit" review generally do not reflect the insistence that you "plow through the entire history of your topic before you dare take a step of your own" (Wolcott, 2001, p. 73).

One of my students once offered this insightful analogy: "Does a restaurant chef demonstrate a command of cooking simply by dumping recipes, unmixed ingredients, and cooking utensils on your table? Tell me, does *that* whet your appetite for what's being offered and instill confidence in what the chef can do?" Better at least to be one of those chefs who comes tableside to concoct the meal, all the while providing lively and precise narration about the selection and contribution of this or that ingredient and spice. That certainly appears the more persuasive way to make your case.

EXAMPLE 9.3   CONCEPTUAL CONTEXT AND THEORETICAL ORIENTATION

As with her Introduction, Patrice got right to the issues at hand in this section of her proposal. She built her conceptual context and theoretical orientation around the three primary currents of thought she had earlier identified: infant mental health, early intervention, and culture theory. This first brief excerpt is her opening paragraph.

This study is informed by the literature and theories related to infant development and early intervention, particularly with the ecological approach to working with families (Dunst, 2000; Dunst, Trivette, & Deal, 1994). In the field of infant development we know that healthy, secure infant attachment is necessary for appropriate overall development for all human babies (Shore, 1997; Small, 1998; Zeanah, 1993). In order for children to endure the challenge of development, which involves risk-taking and inevitable stress, they need to have caregivers who are sensitive and responsive, and who foster a "secure attachment" between infant and caregiver.

The following excerpt illustrates, in one instance, how Patrice perceived that her proposed research fit into (or, rather, addressed gaps in) what was already known in the literature. Again, her intent was not to summarize what had already been done but to ground her proposed inquiry in relevant previous work (Maxwell, 1996). The second paragraph below, in particular, exemplifies what was described in Chapter 4 as a meaningful conceptual linkage between a particular category of knowledge and the problem one was proposing to study. (Note: In the paragraphs preceding this excerpt Patrice had identified and defined the notion of "ecological framework.")

An ecological framework used to understand infant development has proven useful for researchers who are conducting cross-cultural studies and challenging long-held beliefs about normal child development. Small (1998) notes, for example, that "perhaps the most startling finding of ethnopediatrics [anthropological studies of child development] so far is the fact that parenting styles in Western culture—those rules we hold so dear—are not necessarily best for our babies. The parental practices we follow in the West are merely cultural constructions that have little to do with what is 'natural' for babies" (p. xvi). Current researchers are supporting broader understandings of child development, while also challenging long-held assumptions. In particular, that which we know to be valid for many mainstream middle-class American families is not necessarily valid for all children and families, particularly in as plural a society as the United States (Applequist & Bailey, 2000; Halpern, 1993).

Small's claim about the findings of ethnopediatricians, however, rests in the context of infant studies across ethnic and racial boundaries. My proposed study questions how our understanding of infant development can be extended even further across social and economic lines. If ethnopediatrics has uncovered assumptions about "mainstream middle-class American families" relative to ethnically and racially different families, I question the extent to which those same assumptions color our perceptions about the development of infants who grow up in environmentally or economically diverse settings.

Subsequent paragraphs in this section similarly build upon other conceptual linkages Patrice had identified in her earlier efforts to construct a conceptual context for her

---

EXAMPLE 9.3   *continued*

---

inquiry. She then concluded her Conceptual Context section with three paragraphs, each of which focused on a specific current of thought and its linkages to her overall inquiry. Together, these concluding paragraphs provided a bridge to the Research Questions section of her proposal by addressing the essential "so what?" question underlying her discussion thus far: "How does my conceptual context feed into and help to frame my research questions?" You will note in the following excerpts the direct influence of the "If. . . then. . . " propositions she had developed previously (see Chapter 4). I have included only two of the three paragraphs here.

As my questions relate to infant mental health, I question the relationship between social context and infant development. If parents and social groups have differing goals for their children based on the socially determined competencies necessary for survival in a group, then I question what the values and behaviors are of families who live in chronic poverty that adults reward and pass on to their children. Specifically, for families who live in social and economic circumstances different from my own, how do they understand and perceive the well-being of their babies? Do they understand it differently than I do? And do the experiences of infants whose families live in poverty differ significantly from infants whose families do not?

As my questions relate to early intervention, I desire to understand "natural environments" as a function of the social context of early development, in addition to the more apparent physical environment. In order to increase their effectiveness, help givers need to align their efforts with the attitudes, values, and beliefs of the families with whom they partner (Dunst, 2000). The feelings of "disconnect" I personally have experienced partnering with families outside my social experience indicate that I probably do not *understand* them—I do not know life from their perspective. I desire to know how they perceive the world and, in particular, their relationships with the people who are there to "help" them.

Note that Patrice included elements of her personal and professional experience in her discussion. This can be a useful and engaging, but also difficult or even distracting, strategy when constructing your conceptual context. It appears to work in Patrice's case because of how clear the connections are between those experiences and the topics of broader conceptual significance on which she is focused. The key issue in such cases, as Maxwell (1996) reminds us, is not interest, style, or intent, but relevance.

Like a growing number of researchers (Maxwell, 1996; Rossman & Rallis, 1998; Wolcott, 2001), I have become an advocate for critically uncovering rather than exhaustively covering what is relevant and what is problematic among the ideas circling around your inquiry. In a manner that reinforces Maxwell's "ruthless editing" caution near the start of this chapter, Wolcott (2001) likewise urges "sparing" use of citations "and only as the references are critical in helping you analyze and to situate *your* problem and *your* research within some broader context" (p. 75).

Rossman and Rallis (1998) argue further that one's linkage with the literature need not be presented as a separate section of the proposal. "A more lively presentation," they write, "weaves the literature throughout a proposal, drawing on previous research or theoretical concepts to establish what your study is about and how it is likely to contribute to the ongoing dialogue" (p. 74). They suggest building the framework that guides your inquiry within and throughout proposal sections that introduce the topic, situate the problem, and establish the study's significance.

In sum, take ownership of your argument and presentation. Make sure that the concepts and theories in the literature are serving your purposes, not the other way around.

Research Questions

Key Concerns: Focus, Logic

Focus and Purpose of the Research Questions Section

The Research Questions section is the heart of your proposal, the point at which you bring the *focus* and *logic* of your inquiry into clearest definition. Your proposal's Introduction provided a brief preview of your guiding questions, as already noted, and the preceding conceptual section has established a substantial foundation on which your questions can rest. Now is the time to reaffirm and explain the overall coherence of the questions guiding your inquiry. To this end, you will draw most substantially on your prior work in forming and justifying your research questions (Chapter 5). Your research purposes and the conceptual linkages identified in the preceding section serve as supplementary points of reference (see Figure 9.5).

The key to this section's effectiveness is how clearly you connect your questions with each other and with the ideas that motivate and inform them. Let's consider the format that Patrice employed in her proposal. To begin, she stated her questions:

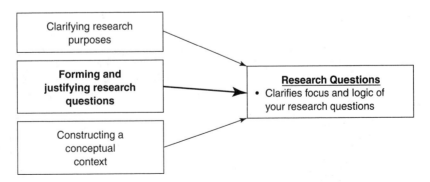

Figure 9.5
Constructing a Justification of Research Questions

The specific questions guiding my research flow directly from the purposes and conceptual argument presented above and are central to my proposed inquiry:
- *What is the meaning of infant well-being from the perspective of families who participate in Early Head Start services?*
- *What is the experience of families who participate in Early Head Start?*

Patrice then offered concise explanations of the intentions and logic underlying each question:

It is important for me to understand infant well-being from the perspective of families because I make an assumption that families who live in social and/or economic circumstances unfamiliar to me value the well-being of their babies, but they value it in a way that I may not understand. This first question positions me to use a cultural interpretation to understand the context of infant development in socially and economically diverse settings. I hope to construct an understanding of how and why these families have the goals and priorities that they do. This understanding can inform service providers' efforts to become more effective helpers.

The second question relates more specifically to the relationship between home visitors and the families with whom they partner and who have different social and economic backgrounds. If families have different goals and priorities for their children based on culturally different ways of raising a baby, then understanding the experience of families' partnerships with home visitors from the perspective of families should illuminate factors that help or hinder these relationships. This knowledge can increase the effectiveness of home visitors as they partner with these families.

She got right to the point: "Here are my questions and this is how they make sense." You can stop at this point or extend your discussion by considering the play of additional subquestions. The power and logic of your central research question(s) can in many cases be enhanced by your ability to convey how they build upon or feed into relevant secondary or surrounding questions. Your basic criterion at this point is coherence, ensuring that your questions form a logically consistent whole, rather "a random collection of queries about your topic" (Maxwell, 1996, p. 107).

Patrice chose to continue her Research Questions section by connecting her primary research questions with sets of secondary questions (the topical questions she had earlier fleshed out, as portrayed in Figure 5.2 in Chapter 5). She wrote:

While there are two central questions driving my research, there are other secondary questions that contribute to my central focus. In order to understand how it is that families understand the well being of their infants, I ask:

At this point she listed the four topical questions listed under her first research question in Figure 5.2. Then she did the same for her second guiding research question:

As I work to understand the experience of families in Early Head Start, my focus is aimed specifically at the relationship between home visitors and families during the process of a family's participation in services. In order to help me understand this relationship, I ask:

At this point she listed the four topical questions listed under her second research question in Figure 5.2.

My advice is to include consideration of such supplemental questions on a when-and-as-needed basis (Wolcott, 2001). Ask yourself: Do they contribute to a clear progression of thought, or will the additional questions simply generate separate (and potentially confusing) clusters of information (Piantanida & Garman, 1999)?

Patrice concluded her Research Questions section with a simple and concise statement of the connectedness among all her questions:

The function of these secondary questions is to "build" an answer to my broader inquiry. While the central questions are grand in scale, the secondary questions pare down the larger questions and tie them more directly and explicitly to my purposes.

In sum, keep *focus* and *logic* in the forefront of your decisions about what and how much to include in the Research Questions section. Make sure that your questions and their respective justifications fit together, build upon one another, and fulfill the intent of your study.

Research Procedures

Key Concerns: Integrity, Credibility, Relationships

Focus and Purpose of the Research Procedures Section

This section of the proposal clarifies and justifies the particular procedural decisions you have made. Rossman and Rallis (1998) suggest that this section should accomplish three major purposes:

- It should present a particular course of action for the conduct of your study.
- It should demonstrate that you are capable of conducting the study.
- It should preserve the design flexibility that is characteristic of qualitative research.

Helping you to address these aims are the strategic, relational, and ethical considerations discussed in Chapters 6, 7, and 8, as well as the issues of perspective and stance described in Chapter 3 (see Figure 9.6). Given the scope and aims of this text, I am assuming that you are drawing upon additional experiences and resources (such as those suggested in Chapter 6) to learn of specific fieldwork methods needed to carry out your research and work with your data.

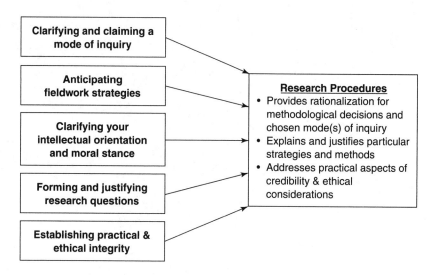

Figure 9.6
Constructing Research Procedures

In suggesting the heading Research Procedures for this section of your proposal, I am following the lead of others (most notably Piantanida & Garman, 1999) whose concerns I share regarding the more common title for this section, Research Methodology or Research Methods. As discussed earlier, *methodology* refers to the theory and analysis of how inquiry does or should proceed and therefore is an inappropriate label for a section that addresses how you are actually going to carry out your study. The term *methods* commonly denotes specific techniques or tools used by the researcher to generate and analyze data. Using Methods as a title is helpful and accurate to a point, but it does not encompass the range of logistical, relational, ethical, and credibility issues that you need to describe in this section of the proposal.

An understanding of Procedures as a *course of action* allows you to incorporate all of the following components (adapted from Glesne, 1999; LeCompte & Schensul, 1999; Maxwell, 1996; Piantanida & Garman, 1999; Rossman & Rallis, 1998):

Description of setting or social context of your study.   Although some choose to make it a separate section prior to Research Procedures, a description is an appropriate way to introduce this section and contextualize your choice of questions and methods. Your identification of the setting, population, or phenomenon of interest conveys the scope and boundedness of your study and thus provides an early indication of whether you are positioned to generate the amount and type of data you need to respond fully to your research questions.

Rossman and Rallis (1998) posit varying levels of constraint and types of obligations placed upon the researcher depending on whether one's research is site specific, population specific, or focused on a phenomenon.

Site-specific research represents a fairly constrained choice in that the study is defined by and closely linked to a particular place. This would have been the case had Patrice's study been focused on a specific Early Head Start center, keeping in mind that this decision would have been predicated on a different research question as well. This type of study requires that you provide significant detail regarding the setting as well as a rationale for why a selected setting might be more appropriate to your question than others.

A *population-specific* study is somewhat less constrained in that it could conceivably be conducted in any number of places. For example, Patrice's study was defined by and linked to participants in Early Head Start, a program with multiple locations and contexts. For this type of study the researcher needs to present a strategy for selecting participants from that population.

A study focused on a particular *phenomenon* is even less constrained by place or population. For example, Patrice might have kept her study at the level of inquiring into the notion of infant well-being without linking it to a particular group or location. This type of focus prompts the researcher to establish an understanding of how the concept or phenomenon of interest might exist across settings or contexts.

Rationale for your research approach.   It is usually necessary to provide a rationale for the research approach or tradition guiding your study. Although this argument can be woven throughout your proposal in ways both explicit (e.g., Patrice's opening statement in the Introduction) and implicit (e.g., Patrice's emphasis on cultural interpretation within her Conceptual Context), you need to convey how your overall approach is appropriate to your inquiry.

The relationship you hope to establish with study participants.   Chapters 7 and 8 highlighted the importance of this dimension of your work, particularly as it pertains to degree and portrayal of involvement, consequences of presence, exchange, disclosure, and other ethical concerns. This is an appropriate section in which to discuss issues of ethics, including procedural matters like informed consent, and less straightforward matters pertaining to research relationships.

Gathering and generating data.   In this part you need to explain how you will get the information you need to respond to your research questions. What kinds of interviews, observations, or other methods do you plan to use, and how will you conduct these? Think of this as the plan that will guide your decisions in the field. It is a demonstration of how you have thought through some of the complexities of fieldwork and formed your initial judgments about how to focus your efforts. This description should also indicate that you have considered the *resource demands* of specific decisions (i.e., "What do I need to accomplish this?").

The most common pitfall in constructing this part of your proposal is the tendency to present the nuts and bolts of gathering data as if such techniques existed in a vacuum without explicating the logical and empirical connections between your research questions, your approach, and your particular methods. "Except in the broadest of terms," cautions Wolcott (1995), "fieldwork techniques cannot be distilled and described independently from the questions that guide the research" (p. 157). You need to make clear to your readers the connections between particular methods and procedures and the data you need to address your questions.

To this end, a number of my students in recent years have found it helpful to construct some version of a *data planning worksheet* or *data collection matrix* as suggested by LeCompte and Schensul (1999; see also LeCompte & Preissle, 1993; Maxwell, 1996). As adapted for use by my students, the primary guiding component of the matrix—what the researcher needs to know—is constructed from topical subquestions that specify anticipated areas for inquiry (refer to Chapter 5 and the Research Questions section of this chapter). Table 9.1 is a hypothetical example of a data collection matrix for Patrice's study of Early Head Start families. (Patrice did not opt for this strategy herself.) For purposes of illustration, I have included an abbreviated sample of her topical questions pertaining to one of her two central research questions.

In developing the data collection section of your proposal, keep in mind that qualitative methods are no longer unknown or in need of exhaustive defense. You need not (and should not) provide a comprehensive and tedious review of the literature about such standard procedures as participant observation and interviewing. Be specific to your study and the significant linkages between your methods and your questions.

Credibility and trustworthiness.   In this section you address head-on the manner in which you are responding to standards for competent performance as a fieldworker, highlighting such issues as researcher presence, the inevitable selectivity of fieldwork, and the play of subjectivity (see Chapter 8). Maxwell (1996) argues persuasively that, especially at the proposal stage, "it is often more important that your reviewers realize that you are *aware* of a particular problem and are thinking about how to deal with it than that you have an airtight plan for solving the problem" (p. 109). He goes on to point out that a critical issue in addressing the credibility issues in your proposal is indicating your openness to and strategies for the examination of competing explanations and discrepant data so that your research does not develop into a self-fulfilling description of events and ideas.

Data management and analysis.   How to articulate at the proposal stage what you will do to make sense of the data you will collect is consistently a top-ranked concern of students. "How can I know *now* what 'chunks' of data are going to be meaningful?" "How can I talk *now* about my emerging understanding of what I will be learning?" "Won't my analysis take shape as I make decisions in the field and uncover important but unanticipated ideas?" All these questions reflect sound reasoning, but the fact remains that you are not a blank analytical slate, even at this preliminary point of inquiry.

Decisions that you have already made up to this point—about your approach, about connections between questions and methods, even about linkages among your conceptual currents—all serve to foreshadow your analytical strategies. Of course you can't draw upon findings you have yet to encounter, but you can draw upon your selected research tradition to address how particular methods of addressing your

Table 9.1
A Data Planning Matrix[1]

Central Question: What is the experience of families who participate in Early Head Start?

What Do I Need to Know? (Topical Subquestions)	Why Do I Need to Know This?	What Kind of Data Will Answer the Question?	Whom Do I Contact for Access?[2]	Projected Timeline & Procedures
Are there implicit goals that home visitors bring to the relationship? If so, what are they?	To clarify values, assumptions, and personal factors on the part of home visitors that may be impacting the relationship	Formal and informal interviews with home visitors; observations of weekly staff meetings; home visitor questionnaire	Jill Smith, EHS Coordinator; EHS home visitors; Liz Jones, EHS administrative assistant	*2001* March–June: Informal interviews; July–Aug.: In-depth interviews; Aug.–Oct.: Observations at EHS center; administer questionnaire
What is the process of relationship building that unfolds between home visitors and their partner families?	To understand how the process unfolds and determine the respective roles played by families and visitors in shaping the relationship	Observations of home visits; informal & formal interviews with families; informal & formal interviews with home visitors	Home visitors: Jan, Bev, Betty, Deb, Kim; Families: Andrews, Mills, Irvins, Gales, Williams	*2001–02* Sept.–Jan.: Participant observation in family homes and at EHS center activities
What meaning do families ascribe to having a home visitor?	To clarify family perceptions and how they compare with visitor perceptions and stated program aims	Informal and formal interviews with families	Families: Andrews, Mills, Irvins, Gales, Williams	*2001* Sept.–Jan.: Participant observation & interviews in family homes *2002* Jan.–March: Follow-up interviews

[1] Adapted from LeCompte and Schensul (1999). This example is based on a select sample of topical subquestions from Patrice's study of families who participate in Early Head Start. A complete matrix would include all of her topical subquestions.

[2] Pseudonyms used for illustrative purposes only.

particular questions likely translate into a particular way (or set of ways) to make sense of what you uncover. For example, Patrice might pose the following types of questions to frame her discussion of data analysis:

- How might ethnography's focus on cultural interpretation shape my interviewing methods and guide my decisions about what is significant in the analysis of interview data?
- What will underlie my decisions about the relative significance of data generated through participant observation and data generated through interviews?
- What types of questions might I ask in order to translate my fieldnotes into a data set?

As in the previous section on data collection, specific examples are more useful to the reader than abstract descriptions. Ownership, focus, and purposefulness, as highlighted near the start of this chapter, should remain your orienting concerns.

Significance and Implications

Key Concerns: Relevance, Claims-Making, Applicability

Focus and Purpose of the Significance and Implications Section

The explicit purpose of this section is to address the "So what?" and "What difference does it make?" questions that readers of your proposal might ask. A less explicit, but no less important, aim of this section is to reaffirm the purposes of your inquiry. Relative to the emphasis given to research purposes in your Introduction, this section of the proposal provides an opportunity to heighten emphasis on the practical aims of your inquiry (see Figure 9.7).

A third, more embedded aim of this section is to convey what you mean by your claims to be "getting at" the focus or topic of your inquiry. Piantanida and Garman (1999) speak of this in terms of students "owning their study," and define this in terms of "embrac[ing] more fully the epistemological assumption that the significance

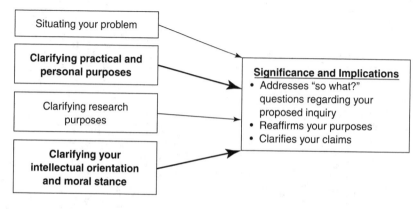

Figure 9.7

Constructing Significance and Implications

of their study lies not within the data per se but in the meaning they make of the data" (p. 145). In other words, maintain perspective on what you *are* claiming (portrayal of your experience with and understanding of a topic) and what you are *not* claiming (discovery or verification of "the truth" about a topic).

A significant dimension of your response to the "so what?" question is your effectiveness in discussing its potential relevance and implications for the broader field of ideas, research, and/or practice in which it is situated. Truth be told, we qualitative researchers would like to have our cake and eat it too: acknowledging the uniqueness of our particular inquiry, but claiming that it is "not so unique that we cannot learn from it and apply its lessons more generally" (Wolcott, 1995, p. 175). Wolcott goes on to highlight the logic and appeal of this both/and stance in the context of providing some helpful advice on how qualitative researchers might respond to questions about the generalizability of their studies. For purposes of illustration, I am inserting Patrice's now familiar study into the guidelines suggested by Wolcott:

- I regard these particular families participating in Early Head Start to be families *in certain respects* like *all* other families participating in Early Head Start.
- I regard these particular families participating in Early Head Start to be families *in certain respects* like *some* other families participating in Early Head Start.
- I regard these particular families participating in Early Head Start to be families *in certain respects* like *no* other families participating in Early Head Start.[1]

If you are challenged by a positivist-oriented committee member about whether a qualitative study is generalizable, you can respond accurately that it is not (in terms that a quantitatively oriented researcher might find acceptable). But as suggested by guidelines like those previously in this chapter and the discussion of context and "complex specificness" in Chapter 1, you need not paint yourself into an either/or corner. Uniqueness or particularity is not the same as isolation; selected aspects of experience can speak to and suggest implications for large or more general issues.

Appendixes

Key Concerns: Extension, Illustration   Appendixes should not simply be an afterthought. They extend and provide supplementary illustration for your proposal argument, without disrupting the flow of the main body of the text. Consider your need for some or all of the following components:

- **A timetable for your research.** This helps readers (and you) judge the feasibility of your proposed study and may suggest questions about logistics and practicality not immediately apparent in the body of your proposal. In

---

[1] Wolcott specifically adapted a statement written decades ago (hence the outmoded gender language) by Kluckholn and Murray to introduce their chapter on personality formation (1948, p. 35):
Every man is in certain respects
a. like all other men,
b. like some other men,
c. like no other man.

some cases, a data planning matrix in the Research Procedures section (e.g., Table 9.1) can serve this purpose. For her proposal, Patrice included a timetable that included not only description of projected research emphases at various points, but also a timeline for periodic updates, or "reconnaissance reports," to her committee members (see Example 9.4).

- **Copies of informed consent forms and/or letters of introduction.**

EXAMPLE 9.4   PROPOSED TIMETABLE

TIMETABLE

Proposed Study: *Infant Well-Being and the Participation of Families in Early Head Start*

March–June 2001

"Reconnaissance"

This will be part-time fieldwork in which I spend time at the Early Head Start center when families are there so that we can get acquainted and start to build trusting relationships. I will be explaining my purpose, obtaining individuals' informed consent to participate, and generally getting a feel for the environment, the relationships, and who among the participants might be "key." During this time I also aim to connect with at least one "prenatal family" so that I will have participants with whom I can have a relationship beginning with their entrance into the program.

Description will focus on the immediate Early Head Start site and interactions within the Early Head Start center.

Informal interviews with staff

Through these interactions I will try to develop an appropriate interview structure and questions for subsequent in-depth interviewing with home visitors.

July–August 2001

Reconnaissance Report I

What are my impressions? Where do I anticipate problems? What have I learned that I haven't expected? Do I need to reconsider my methods or my questions? What is the best way to proceed? Where am I relative to the plan I originally set out?

In-depth interviews with home visiting staff

September 2001–January 2002

Intense fieldwork

There will be a transition period from summer to fall "start up" time when regular programming with Early Head Start begins (August/September). I will also be in the field full time.

In September, description will gradually transition away from the Early Head Start center and staff and move into the daily lives of the families.

EXAMPLE 9.4   *continued*

By mid-winter (January/February) description will move outward from the families into the larger social context of both families and Early Head Start, and into the community as a whole. By this time I expect that I will have a feel for appropriate community informants.

Reconnaissance Report II

Where do I stand in relation to the big picture? How are my methods working for me? Am I learning what I wanted to know? Did my anticipated obstacles and problems pan out? Do I have any new problems? Am I better than half way there? Have I got a plan for writing up? Have I yet explicated patterns of behavior that I can test against my current fieldwork?

Writing up

Writing and continued fieldwork will be happening simultaneously. I should have a rough outline or some ideas about format in the fall. Writing up will be a continual process to be expanded as headnotes, scratchnotes, and fieldnotes get transcribed and coded and as analytic memos unfold.

January–May 2002

Intense writing up. . .

. . . of headnotes scratchnotes, fieldnotes. Continued coding and memoing of all documents. Looking for themes and patterns.

Winding down fieldwork

A gradual pulling away from field relationships. Testing explications of behavior and events. Checking in with participants to make sure that what I have to say is accurate.

Reconnaissance Report III (May)

Where do I stand in relation to the big picture? Has my "trip" been everything that I had expected? If not, why not?

Summer 2002

Dissertation Defense

- **Copy of Institutional Review Board (or similar body) approval for your proposed study.**   Requirements for this vary from institution to institution, as does the expectation that such approval precedes or follows the presentation and defense of your research proposal to a faculty committee or funding agency.
- **Detailed explanation or description of a particular data collection or analysis technique.**   If full explanation of a specific method or technique would take up too much space or disrupt the narrative flow in the body of

the proposal, include it as an appendix. This would also be the place for copies of proposed interview guides or questionnaires.

- **A tentative outline of chapters for your thesis or dissertation.**   Nearly all my students have initially expressed shock at the suggestion of drafting a table of contents before they have even started their research (much as I responded when Harry Wolcott, the chair of my dissertation committee at the University of Oregon, requested the same of me—complete with estimates of the lengths of each chapter!). Like my mentor, however, I have become convinced of the value of this exercise for several reasons (also see Wolcott, 2001). First, this initial attempt to structure what you *think* might be the account you want to develop reveals much about how tightly or loosely you are holding on to certain ideas, theories, and assumptions. To what extent might these ideas be dictating rather than serving your purposes? Second, a draft reveals how constrained (or not) you feel about the structure of the thesis or dissertation itself. Do you feel locked in to the traditional five or six chapter format, and is that format appropriate to the nature and direction of your inquiry? Third, and perhaps most importantly, working through drafts of the table of contents can serve, in similar fashion to the redrafting of titles discussed earlier, as a way to systematically monitor your emerging insights and evolving perspective as a researcher.

Additional Considerations

The framework that I have presented in this chapter is geared toward proposals of roughly 25–30 double-spaced pages, not including appendixes and references (which should be limited to references actually cited in the body of your proposal). This is by no means the only way to organize and present a proposal, but it is one that is responsive to crucial concerns arising out of a thorough conceptualization process. I urge you to attend carefully to variations on this structure that reflect the expectations and requirements of your particular institution or situation.

COMING FULL CIRCLE

If you come away from this book with a sense that your conceptualizing efforts are, by nature and intent, more cumulative than conclusive, then you are well positioned to get on with the task at hand. You have come full circle, engaging with a sense of problem and purpose, communicating the focus of your aims in well-formulated questions, constructing conceptual linkages that lend coherence to your inquiry, arguing for ownership of your ideas, and, finally, staking your claim to follow through on what you want to accomplish.

Generating, accumulating, connecting, paring, and making your case. Together, these actions comprise an iterative process that prefigures your fieldwork and eventual write-up and reveals the inexhaustibility of the conceptualizing task. As suggested by the epigraph that prefaces this book, the real work of qualitative research—the essential mindwork that feeds and reflects back upon your research efforts—continues with no less intensity as you move into the field.

REFERENCES

Agar, M. H. (1996). *The professional stranger: An informal introduction to ethnography* (2nd ed.). San Diego, CA: Academic Press.

Appadurai, A. (1988). Place and voice in anthropological theory. *Cultural Anthropology, 3*(1), 16–20.

Atkinson, P., & Hammersley, M. (1994). Ethnography and participant observation. In N. K. Denzin & Y. S. Lincoln (Eds.), *Handbook of qualitative research* (pp. 248–261). Thousand Oaks, CA: Sage.

Babchuk, W. A. (1997). *The rediscovery of grounded theory: Strategies for qualitative research in adult education.* Unpublished doctoral dissertation, University of Nebraska-Lincoln.

Barone, T. (2001). Science, art, and the predispositions of educational researchers. *Educational Researcher, 30*(7), 24–28.

Behar, R. (1996). *The vulnerable observer.* Boston: Beacon Press.

Benner, P. (Ed.). (1994). *Interpretive phenomenology.* Thousand Oaks, CA: Sage.

Berger, P., & Luckmann, T. (1967). *The social construction of reality.* New York: Anchor.

Bittner, E. (1988). Realism in field research. In R. E. Emerson (Ed.), *Contemporary field research: A collection of readings* (pp. 149–155). Prospect Heights, IL: Waveland.

Bogdan, R., & Biklen, S. K. (1998). *Qualitative research for education : An introduction to theory and methods* (3rd ed.). Boston: Allyn and Bacon.

Brantlinger, E. A. (1999). Inward gaze and activism as moral next steps in inquiry. *Anthropology and Education Quarterly, 30*(4), 413–429.

Brumann, C. (1999). Writing for culture: Why a successful concept should not be discarded. *Current Anthropology, 40*(1), 1–13.

Burke, K. (1935). *Permanence and change.* New York: New Republic.

Bushnell, M. (2001). This bed of roses has thorns: Cultural assumptions and community in an elementary school. *Anthropology and Education Quarterly, 32*(2), 139–166.

Casey, K. (1995, 1996). The new narrative research in education. *Review of Research in Education, 21,* 211–233.

Charmaz, K. (1990). Discovering chronic illness: Using grounded theory. *Social Science Medicine, 30,* 1161–1172.

Charmaz, K. (2000). Grounded theory: Objectivist and constructivist methods. In N. K. Denzin & Y. S. Lincoln (Eds.), *Handbook of qualitative research* (2nd ed., pp. 509–535). Thousand Oaks, CA: Sage.

Charmaz, K. (2002). Qualitative interviewing and grounded theory analysis. In J. F. Gubrium & J. A. Holstein (Eds.), *Handbook of interview research: Context and method.* Thousand Oaks, CA: Sage.

Clandinin, D. J., & Connelly, F. M. (2000). *Narrative inquiry: Experience in story in qualitative research.* San Francisco: Jossey-Bass.

Coffey, A., & Atkinson, P. (1996). *Making sense of qualitative data.* Thousand Oaks, CA: Sage.

Cortazzi, M. (1993). *Narrative analysis.* Bristol, PA: Falmer Press.

Creswell, J. W. (1998). *Qualitative inquiry and research design: Choosing among five traditions.* Thousand Oaks, CA: Sage.

Creswell, J. W. (2002). *Educational research: Planning, conducting, and evaluating quantitative and qualitative research.* Upper Saddle River, NJ: Merrill/Prentice Hall.

Creswell, J. W., & Miller, D. L. (2000). Determining validity in qualitative inquiry. *Theory into Practice, 39*(3), 124–130.

de Laine, M. (2000). *Fieldwork, participation and practice: Ethics and dilemmas in qualitative research.* Thousand Oaks, CA: Sage.

Denzin, N. K. (1997). *Interpretive ethnography: Ethnographic practices for the 21ˢᵗ century.* Thousand Oaks, CA: Sage.

Denzin, N. K., & Lincoln, Y. S. (1994). Introduction: Entering the field of qualitative research. In N. K. Denzin & Y. S. Lincoln (Eds.), *Handbook of qualitative research* (pp. 1–17). Thousand Oaks, CA: Sage.

Deyhle, D. L., Hess, G. A., & LeCompte, M. D. (1992). Approaching ethical issues for qualitative researchers in education. In M. LeCompte, W. L. Millroy, & J. Preissle (Eds.), *Handbook of qualitative research in education* (pp. 597–641). San Diego, CA: Academic Press.

Dickens, D., & Fontana, A. (Eds.). (1994). *Postmodernism and social inquiry.* New York: Guilford Press.

Dolby, N. (2000). The significance of place: Fieldwork reflections on "South Africa" and "the United States." *Anthropology and Education Quarterly, 31*(4), 486–492.

Edson, C. H. (1988). Our past and present: Historical inquiry in education. In R. R. Sherman & R. B. Webb (Eds.), *Qualitative research in education: Focus and methods* (pp. 44–58). Bristol, PA: Falmer Press.

Eisner, E. W. (1998). *The enlightened eye: Qualitative inquiry and the enhancement of educational practice.* Upper Saddle River, NJ: Merrill/Prentice Hall.

Eliot, T. S. (1950). *Selected essays.* New York: Harcourt Brace.

Emerson, R. M., Fretz, R. I., & Shaw, L. L. (1995). *Writing ethnographic fieldnotes.* Chicago: University of Chicago Press.

Emihovich, C. (1999). Studying schools, studying ourselves: Ethnographic perspectives on educational reform. *Anthropology and Education Quarterly, 30*(4), 477–483.

Erickson, F. (1984). What makes school ethnography ethnographic? *Anthropology and Education Quarterly, 15*(1), 51–66.

Erickson, F. (1986). Qualitative methods in research on teaching. In M. C. Wittrock (Ed.), *Handbook of research on teaching* (3ʳᵈ ed., pp. 119–161). New York: Macmillan.

Esteva, G., & Prakash, M. S. (1998). *Grassroots postmodernism.* New York: Zed Books.

Farganis, S. (1994). Postmodernism and feminism. In D. Dickens & A. Fontana (Eds.), *Postmodernism and social inquiry* (pp. 101–126). New York: Guilford Press.

Ferrini-Mundy, J., & Schram, T. (Eds.). (1997). Recognizing and recording reform in mathematics education: Issues and implications. *Journal of Research in Mathematics Education* Monograph No. 8. Reston, VA: National Council of Teachers of Mathematics.

Flinders, D. J. (1992). In search of ethical guidance: Constructing a basis for dialogue. *International Journal of Qualitative Studies in Education, 5*(2), 101–115.

Flinders, D. J., & Mills, G. E. (1993). *Theory and concepts in qualitative research: Perspectives from the field.* New York: Teachers College Press.

Fontana, A. (1994). Ethnographic trends in the postmodern era. In D. Dickens & A. Fontana (Eds.), *Postmodernism and social inquiry* (pp. 203–223). New York: Guilford Press.

Geertz, C. (1973). *The interpretation of cultures.* New York: Basic Books.

Geertz, C. (1984). On the nature of anthropological understanding. In R. A. Shweder & R. A. LeVine (Eds.), *Culture theory: Essays on mind, self, and emotion.* New York: Cambridge University Press.

Giorgi, A. (1994). A phenomenological perspective on certain qualitative research methods. *Journal of Phenomenological Psychology, 25,* 190–220.

Giorgi, A. (1997). The theory, practice, and evaluation of the phenomenological methods as a qualitative research procedure. *Journal of Phenomenological Studies, 28*(2), 235–281.

Glaser, B. G. (1978). *Theoretical sensitivity.* Mill Valley, CA: Sociology Press.

Glaser, B. G. (1992). *Basics of grounded theory analysis.* Mill Valley, CA: Sociology Press.

Glaser, B. G., & Strauss, A. (1967). *The discovery of grounded theory.* Chicago: Aldine.

Glesne, C. (1989). Rapport and friendship in ethnographic research. *International Journal of Qualitative Studies in Education, 2*(1), 45–54.

Glesne, C. (1999). *Becoming qualitative researchers: An introduction* (2ⁿᵈ ed.). White Plains, NY: Longman.

Glesne, C., & Peshkin, A. (1992). *Becoming qualitative researchers: An introduction.* White Plains, NY: Longman.

Goetz, J. P., & LeCompte, M. D. (1984). *Ethnography and qualitative design in educational research.* New York: Academic Press.

Guba, E. G., & Lincoln, Y. S. (1994). Competing paradigms in qualitative research. In N. K. Denzin & Y. S. Lincoln (Eds.), *Handbook of qualitative research* (pp. 105–117). Thousand Oaks, CA: Sage.

Hammersley, M. (1990). *Reading ethnographic research: A critical guide.* New York: Longman.

Hess, G. A. (1999). Keeping educational anthropology relevant: Asking good questions rather than trivial ones. *Anthropology and Education Quarterly, 30*(4), 404–412.

Holstein, J. A., & Gubrium, J. F. (1994). Phenomenology, ethnomethodology, and interpretive practice. In N. K. Denzin & Y. S. Lincoln (Eds.), *Handbook of qualitative research* (pp. 262–272). Thousand Oaks, CA: Sage.

Janesick, V. J. (1994). The dance of qualitative research design: Metaphor, methodolatry, and meaning. In N. K. Denzin & Y. S. Lincoln (Eds.), *Handbook of qualitative research* (pp. 209–219). Thousand Oaks, CA: Sage.

Jansen, G., & Peshkin, A. (1992). Subjectivity in qualitative research. In M. LeCompte, W. L. Millroy, & J. Preissle (Eds.), *Handbook of qualitative research in education* (pp. 681–725). San Diego, CA: Academic Press.

Kellehear, A. (1993). *The unobtrusive researcher: A guide to methods.* Sydney: Allen and Unwin.

Kincheloe, J. L., & McLaren, P. L. (1994). Rethinking critical theory and qualitative research. In N. K. Denzin & Y. S. Lincoln (Eds.), *Handbook of qualitative research* (pp. 138–157). Thousand Oaks, CA: Sage.

Kluckholn, C., & Murray, H. A. (1948). *Personality in nature, society, and culture.* New York: Alfred A. Knopf.

Kuper, A. (1999). *Culture: The anthropologists' account.* Cambridge, MA: Harvard University Press.

Lareau, A. (1989). *Home advantage: Social class and parental intervention in elementary education.* New York: Falmer.

LeCompte, M. D., & Preissle, J. P., with Tesch, R. (1993). *Ethnography and qualitative design in educational research* (2nd ed.). San Diego, CA: Academic Press.

LeCompte, M. D., & Schensul, J. J. (1999). *Designing and conducting ethnographic research.* Walnut Creek, CA: AltaMira Press.

LeCompte, M. D., Schensul, J. J., Weeks, M. R., & Singer, M. (1999). *Researcher roles and research partnerships.* Walnut Creek, CA: AltaMira Press.

Lincoln, Y. S. (1995). The sixth moment: Emerging problems in qualitative research. *Studies in Symbolic Interactionism, 19,* 37–55.

Lincoln, Y. S., & Guba, E. G. (2000). Paradigmatic controversies, contradictions, and emerging confluences. In N. K. Denzin & Y. S. Lincoln (Eds.), *Handbook of qualitative research* (2nd ed., pp. 163–188). Thousand Oaks, CA: Sage.

Magolda, P. M. (2000). The campus tour: Ritual and community in higher education. *Anthropology and Education Quarterly, 31*(1), 24–36.

Maguire, P. (1996). Considering more feminist participatory research: What's congruency got to do with it? *Qualitative Inquiry, 2*(1), 106–118.

Marshall, C., & Rossman, G. B. (1999). *Designing qualitative research* (3rd ed.). Thousand Oaks, CA: Sage.

Maxwell, J. A. (1992). Understanding and validity in qualitative research. *Harvard Educational Review, 62*(3), 279–300.

Maxwell, J. A. (1996). *Qualitative research design: An interactive approach.* Thousand Oaks, CA: Sage.

Merriam, S. B. (1998). *Qualitative research and case study applications in education.* San Francisco: Jossey-Bass.

Metz, M. H. (2000). Sociology and qualitative methodologies in educational research. *Harvard Educational Review, 70*(1), 60–74.

Miles, M. B., & Huberman, A. M. (1994). *Qualitative data analysis* (2nd ed.). Thousand Oaks, CA: Sage.

Mills, C. W. (1959). On intellectual craftsmanship. In C. W. Mills (Ed.), *The sociological imagination* (pp. 195–226). London: Oxford University Press.

Mills, G. (2000). Action research: A guide for the teacher researcher. Upper Saddle River, NJ: Merrill/Prentice Hall.

Mishler, E. G. (1979). Meaning in context: Is there any other kind? *Harvard Education Review, 49*(1), 1–19.

Morse, J. M. (1994). Designing funded qualitative research. In N. K. Denzin & Y. S. Lincoln (Eds.), *Handbook of qualitative research* (pp. 220–235). Thousand Oaks, CA: Sage.

Moustakas, C. (1994). *Phenomenological research methods.* Thousand Oaks, CA: Sage.

Page, R. N. (2000). The turn inward in qualitative research. *Harvard Educational Review, 70*(1), 23–38.

Patton, M. Q. (2002). *Qualitative research and evaluation methods* (3rd ed.). Thousand Oaks, CA: Sage.

Peacock, J. L. (1986). *The anthropological lens: Harsh light, soft focus.* New York: Cambridge University Press.

Peshkin, A. (1984). Odd man out: The participant observer in an absolutist setting. *Sociology of Education, 57,* 254–264.

Peshkin, A. (1985). From title to title: The evolution of perspective in qualitative inquiry. *Anthropology and Education Quarterly, 16*(3), 214–224.

Peshkin, A. (1988). In search of subjectivity—One's own. *Educational Researcher, 17*(7), 17–21.

Peshkin, A. (2000). The nature of interpretation in qualitative research. *Educational Researcher, 29*(9), 5–9.

Piantanida, M., & Garman, N. B. (1999). *The qualitative dissertation: A guide for students and faculty.* Thousand Oaks, CA: Corwin Press.

Poggie, J. J., Jr., DeWalt, B. R., & Dressler, W. W. (Eds.). (1992). *Anthropological research: Process and application.* Albany: State University of New York Press.

Polkinghorne, D. E. (1989). Phenomenological research methods. In R. S. Valle & S. Halling (Eds.), *Existential-phenomenological perspectives in psychology* (pp. 41–60). New York: Plenum.

Punch, M. (1994). Politics and ethics in qualitative research. In N. K. Denzin & Y. S. Lincoln (Eds.), *Handbook of qualitative research* (pp. 83–97). Thousand Oaks, CA: Sage.

Ray, M. A. (1994). The richness of phenomenology: Philosophic, theoretic, and methodologic concerns. In J. M. Morse (Ed.), *Critical issues in qualitative research methods* (pp. 117–133). Thousand Oaks, CA: Sage.

Richardson, L. (1994). Writing: A method of inquiry. In N. K. Denzin & Y. S. Lincoln (Eds.), *Handbook of qualitative research* (pp. 516–529). Thousand Oaks, CA: Sage.

Robbins, T. (1980). *Still life with a woodpecker: A sort of love story.* New York: Bantam Books.

Rogers, L. J., & Swadener, B. B. (1999). Reframing the "field." *Anthropology and Education Quarterly, 30*(4), 436–440.

Rossman, G. B., & Rallis, S. F. (1998). *Learning in the field: An introduction to qualitative research.* Thousand Oaks, CA: Sage.

Salvio, P., & Schram, T. (1995). Making the familiar strange: Learning within and beyond one's cultural borders. *Teaching and Learning: The Journal of Natural Inquiry, 9*(3), 30–39.

Sanjek, R. (1991). On ethnographic validity. In R. Sanjek (Ed.), *Fieldnotes: The makings of anthropology* (pp. 385–418). Ithaca, NY: Cornell University Press.

Schensul, S., Schensul, J. J., & LeCompte, M. D. (1999). *Essential ethnographic methods: Observations, interviews, and questionnaires.* Walnut Creek, CA: AltaMira.

Schram, T. (1993). Laotian refugees in a small-town school: Contexts and encounters. *Journal of Research in Rural Education, 9*(3), 125–136.

Schram, T. (1994). Players along the margin: Diversity and adaptation in a lower track classroom. In Spindler, G., & Spindler, L. (Eds.), *Pathways to cultural awareness: Cultural therapy with teachers and students* (pp. 61–91). Thousand Oaks, CA: Corwin.

Schram, T. (2000). *Extending ethnographic intent: What we do with what we know.* Paper presented at the annual meeting of the American Educational Research Association Annual Meeting, New Orleans, Louisiana.

Schutz, A. (1967). *The phenomenology of the social world.* Evanston, IL: Northwestern University Press.

Schutz, A. (1970). *On phenomenology and social relations.* Chicago: University of Chicago Press.

Schwandt, T. A. (1993). Theory for the moral sciences: Crisis of identity and purpose. In D. J. Flinders & G. E. Mills (Eds.), *Theory and concepts in qualitative research: Perspectives from the field* (pp. 5–23). New York: Teachers College Press.

Schwandt, T. A. (1994). Constructivist, interpretivist approaches to human inquiry. In N. K. Denzin & Y. S. Lincoln (Eds.), *Handbook of qualitative research* (pp. 118–137). Thousand Oaks, CA: Sage.

Schwandt, T. A. (1995). Thoughts on the moral career of the interpretive inquirer. *Studies in Symbolic Interactionism, 19,* 131–140.

Schwandt, T. A. (1997). *Qualitative inquiry: A dictionary of terms.* Thousand Oaks, CA: Sage.

Schwandt, T. A. (2000). Three epistemological stances for qualitative inquiry: Interpretivism, hermeneutics, and social constructivism. In N. K. Denzin & Y. S. Lincoln (Eds.), *Handbook of qualitative research* (2nd ed., pp. 189–214). Thousand Oaks, CA: Sage.

Seidel, J. (1992). Method and madness in the application of computer technology to qualitative data analysis. In N. G. Fielding & R. M. Lee (Eds.), *Using computers in qualitative research* (pp. 107–116). Newbury Park, CA: Sage.

Seidman, I. (1998). *Interviewing as qualitative research: A guide for researchers in education and the social sciences* (2nd ed.). New York: Teachers College Press.

Spindler, G., & Spindler, L. (1982). *Doing the ethnography of schooling.* New York: Holt, Rinehart and Winston.

Stake, R. E. (1995). *The art of case study research.* Thousand Oaks, CA: Sage.

Stewart, D., & Mickunas, A. (1990). *Exploring phenomenology: A guide to the field and its literature* (2nd ed.). Athens: Ohio University Press.

Strauss, A. (1987). *Qualitative analysis for social scientists.* New York: Cambridge University Press.

Strauss, A., & Corbin, J. (1994). Grounded theory methodology: An overview. In N. K. Denzin & Y. S. Lincoln (Eds.), *Handbook of qualitative research* (pp. 273–285). Thousand Oaks, CA: Sage.

Strauss, A., & Corbin, J. (1998). *Basics of qualitative research: Techniques and procedures for developing grounded theory* (2nd ed.). Thousand Oaks, CA: Sage.

Taylor, S. J. & Bogdan, R. (1984). *An introduction to qualitative research: The search for meanings* (2nd ed.). New York: Wiley.

Tesch, R. (1990). *Qualitative research: Analysis types and software tools.* London: Falmer.

Van Maanen, J. (1988). *Tales of the field: On writing ethnography.* Chicago: The University of Chicago Press.

Van Manen, M. (1990). *Researching lived experience: Human science for an action sensitive pedagogy.* London, ON: Althouse.

Watkins, J. M. (2001). Researching researchers and teachers: Comment on "not talking past each other." *Anthropology and Education Quarterly, 32*(3), 379–387.

Wolcott, H. F. (1988). "Problem finding" in qualitative research. In H. Trueba & C. Delgado-Gaitan (Eds.), *School and society: Learning content through culture* (pp. 11–35). New York: Praeger.

Wolcott, H. F. (1990). Making a study more ethnographic. *Journal of Contemporary Ethnography, 19*(1), 44–72.

Wolcott, H. F. (1992). Posturing in qualitative inquiry. In M. LeCompte, W. L. Millroy, & J. Preissle (Eds.), *Handbook of qualitative research in education* (pp. 3–52). San Diego, CA: Academic Press.

Wolcott, H. F. (1994). *Transforming qualitative data: Description, analysis, and interpretation.* Thousand Oaks, CA: Sage.

Wolcott, H. F. (1995). *The art of fieldwork.* Walnut Creek, CA: AltaMira.

Wolcott, H. F. (1999). *Ethnography: A way of seeing.* Walnut Creek, CA: AltaMira.

Wolcott, H. F. (2001). *Writing up qualitative research* (2nd ed.). Thousand Oaks, CA: Sage.

Yin, R. K. (1994). *Case study research: Design and methods.* Thousand Oaks, CA: Sage.

Zigo, D. (2001). Rethinking reciprocity: Collaboration in labor as a path toward equalizing power in classroom research. *International Journal of Qualitative Studies in Education, 14*(3), 351–365.

INDEX

Agar, M. H., 7, 21, 34, 41, 67, 68, 69
Analytic memo, 20
Appadurai, A., 34
Appendixes, 111, 131–134
Applicability, 130–131
Arguments
    formulating, 44–45
    for qualitative research proposals, 110, 112
Assumptions, 57–58
    ethnographic, 68
    grounded theory, 74
    phenomenological, 71
Atkinson, P., 67
Attention, 78
Attentiveness, 9, 11
Authority, 44

Babchuk, W. A., 73
Barone, T., 6
Becker, Howard, 14
Behar, R., 40, 99
Behavior
    cultural, 67
    phenomenology and, 71
Beliefs, 30–32
Benner, P., 70
Berger, P., 33
Biklen, S. K., 56
Bittner, E., 96
Bogdan, R., 56, 90
Boundary spanning, 103
Boundedness, 59
Brantlinger, E. A., 25–26, 33
Breadth, 49, 50–52, 56–57
Brumann, C., 67
Burke, Kenneth, 65
Bushnell, M., 34

Case study, 2
Casey, K., 66
Chapter outline, 134
Charmaz, K., 72, 73–74, 75
Circumstantial selectivity, 98
Claims-making, 130–131
Clandinin, D. J., 3, 66
Coherence, 41, 119–120
Complex specificness, 9
Comprehensiveness, 44
Conceptual context, 41–47, 111, 119–123
Conceptual density, 75
Conceptual integrity, 41
Conceptualization, 10–11, 109–110, 111
Conceptual significance, 112
Connectedness, 42
Connelly, F. M., 3, 66
Consequential presence, 97
Constant comparison, 75
Constructivist design, 73
Contested paradigms, 33
Context, 93
    conceptual, 41–47, 111, 119–123
    personal, 117–118
    sensitivity to, 8–9, 11
    social, 126–127
Contextualization, 69
Conversations, qualitative, 2–5
Corbin, J., 22, 72, 73, 74, 75
Cortazzi, M., 3, 66
Course of action, 126
Credibility, 45, 125–130
Creswell, J. W., 14, 30, 52, 53, 57, 66, 72, 73–74, 77, 98
Critical paradigm, 34–35

Critical theory, 34
Critique, 42
Cultural behaviors, 67
Culture, 68–69, 76
Currents of thought, 45, 120
Cycle of inquiry, 14

Data collection and generation, 127–128, 129, 133–134
Data management and analysis, 128, 130, 133–134
Data planning worksheet/data collection matrix, 128, 129
Deal, 121
Deductive, 21
Degree, of involvement, 89–90
de Laine, M., 4, 39
Denzin, N. K., 4, 39
Descriptive aims, 25
Descriptive questions, 60
Design
    constructivist, 73
    emergent, 21, 73
    research, 14–15
    systematic, 73
DeWalt, B. R., 36
Deyhle, D. L., 103
Dichotomizing conversation, 4–5
Dickens, D., 4
Disciplinary conversation, 3
Disclosure, 101, 103–105
Dolby, N., 88
Dressler, W. W., 36
Durkheim, Emily, 36

Ecological paradigm, 36–37
Edson, C. H., 10
Eliot, T. S., 58